Depth

Immigration Nation

Aaron Wilkes

OXFORD
UNIVERSITY PRESS

OXFORD
UNIVERSITY PRESS

Great Clarendon Street, Oxford OX2 6DP

Oxford University Press is a department of the University of Oxford.

It furthers the University's objective of excellence in research, scholarship, and education by publishing worldwide in Oxford
New York   Auckland   Cape Town   Dar es Salaam   Hong Kong
Karachi   Kuala Lumpur   Madrid   Melbourne   Mexico City
Nairobi   New Delhi   Shanghai   Taipei   Toronto

With offices in
Argentina   Austria   Brazil   Chile   Czech Republic   France   Greece
Guatemala   Hungary   Italy   Japan   Poland   Portugal   Singapore
South Korea   Switzerland   Thailand   Turkey   Ukraine   Vietnam

Oxford is a registered trade mark of Oxford University Press
in the UK and in certain other countries

British Library Cataloguing in Publication Data

Data available

ISBN 978-1-85008-559-1

10 9 8 7 6 5 4 3 2 1

Printed in Spain by Cayfosa-Impresia Ibérica

Acknowledgements

Text design and layout: Sally Boothroyd

Illustrators: Clive Wakfer and Tony Randell

Cover design: Sally Boothroyd and Rosa Capacchione

Cover images: © Clive Chilvers/Shutterstock, Image Source/Corbis, Bettmann/Corbis

Aaron Wilkes wishes to thank Jennifer Harwood and Minh Ha Duong for all their hard work and advice. He would also like to thank Emma Wilkes for all her patience and good humour during the preparation of this book.

The author and publisher are grateful to the following for permission to reprint copyright material:

Extract from Home Office 'Life in the UK' sample tests is Crown © copyright, and is used under the terms of the Open Government Licence.

British Sky Broadcasting Ltd for extract from Graham Fitzgerald: '60,000 asylum seekers lost without trace', *Sky News*, 11.1.2011.

Express Syndication for extract from table in Jo Willey: 'The Best of British', The Daily Express, 24.6.2008, copyright © Express Newspapers 2008.

Guardian News & Media Ltd for extracts from From our Special Correspondent : 'Why 492 West Indians came to Britain', *The Guardian* 23.6.1948, copyright © Guardian News & Media Ltd 1948; and Adam Roberts: 'More Migrants Please', *The Guardian*, 4.1.2008, copyright © Guardian News & Media Ltd 2008.

Hodder Education for extract from J D Clare: *A Nation of Immigrants* (Hodder, 2010), copyright © J D Clare 2010.

Little, Brown Book Group Ltd for extracts from John Winder: *Bloody Foreigners* (Abacus, 2004).

Penguin Books Ltd for Benjamin Zephaniah: 'The British (serves 60 million)' from *Wicked World* (Puffin Poetry, 2000), copyright © Benjamin Zephaniah 2000.

Telegraph Media Group for extract from Philip Johnson: 'Record Immigration sees UK Population Soar', *The Daily Telegraph*, 23.10.2007, copyright © Telegraph Media Group Ltd 2007.

Contents

What is history?

Before you start this book, take a few minutes to think about these questions.

- What do you think history is? What does the word mean?
- What have you learnt in history lessons before, perhaps in your primary school or in other years at secondary school? Did you enjoy them or not? If you enjoyed them, say why. If you didn't enjoy them, why not?
- Have you read any history books or stories about things that happened a long time ago? Have you watched any television programmes, films or plays about things that happened in the past? If so, which ones?

History is about what happened in the past. It is about people in the past, what they did and why they did it, what they thought and what they felt. To enjoy history you need to have a good imagination. You need to be able to imagine what life was like in the past, or what it may have been like to be involved in past events.

How did people feel, think and react to events like these?

The year is 1290 and King Edward is expelling us Jews from England. Yet we have contributed so much to this country! Some of its most beautiful cathedrals would not be here without the money we lent to church leaders, and we've helped pay for armies to defend England. But now King Edward has said we have to leave, so he can claim all our land, money and property. But will he *really* go through with it? What if we refuse to go? And if we leave, how long before we can come back... if ever?

It is 1918 and I've just spent four years fighting for Britain. I was born and bred in India but when the Great War broke out thousands of us joined the British Army. By the end of 1914, one in three soldiers fighting for Britain in France was Indian. We won 13,000 medals between us – and Britain couldn't have won the war without us. Now I want to settle in Britain and bring my family over from India. I've told them how free and fair Britain is. Surely I'll be welcomed as a war hero who has done their bit... won't I?

I think we've let too many immigrants into Britain recently. Where we live, it's like we're foreigners in our own country! They come to take our jobs, use our hospitals and fill up our schools. I'm not being racist, but I do think the government should stop foreigners coming here and draining this nation. We're already a crowded country and we just can't afford any more immigrants. Is there a political party I can vote for that wants to stop immigration altogether?

How to use this book

As you work through this book, you will notice a number of features that keep appearing.

MISSION OBJECTIVES

MISSION ACCOMPLISHED?

All sections of this book will start by setting your Mission Objectives. These are your key aims that set out your learning targets for the work ahead. Topics will end by trying to get you to assess your own learning. If you can accomplish each Mission Objective then you are doing well!

WISE-UP Words

WISE-UP Words are key terms that are vital to help you discuss and understand the topics. You can spot them easily because they are in bold type. Look up their meanings in a dictionary or use the Glossary at the end of the book. The Glossary is a list of words and their meanings.

PAUSE for Thought

Some topics contain PAUSE for Thought boxes. This is an opportunity for you to stop and think for yourself.

Hungry for MORE

The Hungry for MORE features give you a chance to extend your knowledge and research beyond the classroom. This is a time for you to take responsibility for your own learning. You might be asked to research something in the library or on the Internet, work on a presentation, or design and make something. Can you meet the challenge?

FACT

These are all the fascinating, amazing or astounding little bits of history that you usually don't get to hear about! But we think they are just as important and give you insights into topics that you'll easily remember.

BIG QUESTION

This book will ask you to consider some of the 'Big Questions' about immigration to Britain. It will encourage you to think about why people came to Britain from different countries, what happened to them when they got here and how immigration has changed Britain.

DEPTH STUDY

There are also three Depth Studies in this book. These will get you to focus on the following themes:

- **JEWISH IMMIGRATION**
- **BLACK IMMIGRATION**
- **SOUTH ASIAN IMMIGRATION**

These Depth Studies focus on key groups of immigrants from around the world who have had an important impact on Britain.

Work

Work sections are your opportunity to demonstrate your knowledge and understanding. You might be asked to put events in the correct chronological order. You might be asked to:

- explain how things have changed over time
- work out why two people might interpret the same event differently
- work out what triggered an event to take place in the short term or the long term.

Why should we study immigration?

The topic of immigration is one of the most fascinating and significant in the story of Britain. It is also deeply controversial, incredibly divisive and very relevant in today's world. In fact, it's everything a good history topic should be! So what is it about the story of immigration that makes it so important?

The immigration story tells us a lot about history

By studying the different groups of people who came to settle in Britain, you learn a lot about the different places they came from. You learn even more about the country they came to, the attitudes of the people who already lived in Britain at the time, and the contribution the immigrants made in terms of culture, ideas and wealth.

> 'History should not all be about Kings and Queens, dates and battles, but should look at how immigration is firmly entwined with any notion of what it is to be British.'

↰ **SOURCE A:** *Politician Barbara Roche in an article called 'Beat the Backlash', 2004.*

Immigration has had a huge impact on Britain

There is no doubt at all that immigration has had a major effect on this nation, and as historians it is important that we understand this.

> 'No-one with any knowledge of the immense contribution, both economic and cultural, that immigrants and their descendants have made to Britain in the past could possibly doubt that, without it, Britain would lack much that makes it the country it is today. Indeed, much of what is thought of as British has been contributed by them. From Punch and Judy to Madame Tussaud's, from Selfridges to Marks & Spencer, from Handel's 'Water Music' to the poetry of John Betjeman, and not least that pair of fictitious characters Ali G and Vicky Pollard. So much of what today forms part of the country's cultural landscape is owed to immigrants or their descendants, that it is hard to imagine how Britain might have been today were it not to have received any immigration.'

↰ **SOURCE B:** *From an article called* A nation of Immigrants? *by David Conway, 2007. In it he lists different things that we think of as British, which have actually been brought to Britain or created by immigrants or their descendants. Ali G and Vicky Pollard, for example, are two fictional comedy characters created by Sacha Baron Cohen (son of a Jewish immigrant mother) and Matt Lucas (the descendant of Jewish immigrants).*

Immigration is important in the present and future too

Immigration has been an important topic in the past, is an important topic today, and will continue to be important in the future. It has been an issue throughout the centuries, in all sorts of ways and for all sorts of people. Queen Elizabeth I, for example, felt that there were 'too manie' black immigrants in 1596 – and in 1723 a newspaper article argued that the amount of immigrants must be limited or London would 'swarm with them'! Immigration continues to be a 'hot topic' in workplaces, homes, schools and parliament today, and will be for years to come (see Source C).

RECORD IMMIGRATION SEES UK POPULATION SOAR

Record immigration is fuelling the biggest rise in population for almost 50 years, official figures show. Ten years from now, there will be 65 million people in the UK – an increase of five million – and by 2031, the population will be over 70 million, the Office for National Statistics (ONS) said. Within a generation, immigration will add the equivalent of a city the size of London to the population. Statisticians said at least 70% of the population rise over the next 20 years will be directly due to immigration…'

↰ **SOURCE C:** *From an article in the* Daily Telegraph, *23 October 2007.*

What do you think of the statement: 'There are too many immigrants?'

- Strongly disagree
- Don't know
- Strongly agree
- Tend to agree
- Neither nor
- Tend to disagree

Should the government encourage immigrants to leave Britain?

- Don't know
- Refused
- Should
- Should not

↰ **SOURCE D:** *From a* **MORI poll,** *April 2008. In total, 1000 people were interviewed, selected from a wide-ranging sample of the British public. The results clearly show how divided Britain is over the topic of immigration.*

The topic of immigration promotes debate

Nearly everybody has an opinion on immigration. During election times, for example, immigration is often one of the most talked about issues. In the 2010 General Election, immigration was one of the top three issues that voters were most interested in (the other two were the economy and the health service). It's a topic that clearly matters a lot in the lives of ordinary Britons, so it is very important that young people know as much as they can about immigration. Only then can they form their own opinion on such a key issue.

WISE-UP Words
immigration
MORI poll

Immigration is a fascinating topic

Let's not forget one of the best reasons to study the topic of immigration – because it is a thoroughly absorbing story of bravery, adventure, violence, humour, hard work… and lots more!

SOURCE E: *The Tottenham Hotspur Football Club team photograph of 1909. You may notice one black face in the team – his name was Walter Tull and he was Britain's first black outfield professional footballer. He was also the first black officer in the British Army, and he fought (and died) for Britain in World War One. He was the son of an immigrant and the grandson of a slave. His story is fascinating… and is a great example of how interesting the topic of immigration can be!* ↳

Tottenham Hotspur Football Club, 1911-12.

JONES BROS
708 HIGH RD
TOTTENHAM

Immigration tells us a lot about modern Britain

It is often said that Britain is a multicultural country. The study of immigration helps you understand why. The topic is very personal to some people too – it may be that you or some of your classmates are yourselves part of the immigration story. Approaching the topic sensibly, sensitively and with an open mind will help you better understand the different races and cultures in your school, your community and your country.

↳ **SOURCE F:** *Britain's schools are a good example of 'Multicultural Britain'. Here, Queen Elizabeth II visits a school in London.*

What's what and who's who?

It is vital to know exactly what particular key words and phrases mean when studying immigration. So: *an immigrant is someone who comes to live in Britain from another country.* They could be:

A) A citizen of the European Union (EU). In 2010 there were 27 countries (called member states) in the EU (see Source G). Anyone from an EU country can go and live and work in any other EU country. So a Lithuanian builder has just as much right to work in Britain as a British teacher has to go and work in Spain!

B) A person from a country outside the EU who has permission to be here. This could include '**economic migrants**', who come to Britain to work. In recent years the government has used a points system that gives different amounts of points based on a potential immigrant's skills, education, age etc. The younger, more skilled, better educated immigrants are given more points – and the more points an immigrant has, the more chance they have of being granted permission (called a **visa**) to stay.

↳ **SOURCE G:** *The 27 member states of the European Union. A further nine countries have applied to join. The EU is like a big club of countries, which share certain rules, regulations, laws and so on. Some of the EU countries even share the same currency – the euro.*

BBC News: Immigration points system begins

The government launched the first stage of a new points-based system for migrants from outside the EU today. The system is designed to make it easier for highly skilled workers to enter the UK, but more difficult for those with fewer or lower skills. It is similar to schemes used in Canada and Australia, where foreigners win points for factors including qualifications, work experience and language skills. Under the new system, skilled workers in occupations where there is a shortage will also be able to enter, provided they have a job offer.

↳ **SOURCE H:** *From a BBC Online article, February 2008.*

C) An 'asylum seeker' who has fled to Britain to avoid war, natural disasters or persecution in their own country. When a person seeks asylum in Britain they have to prove they are in danger in their own country to have a chance of being given permission to stay. They are not permitted to work while their asylum application is being considered. There are currently around 20,000–30,000 asylum applications each year, and in 2007, for example, only 26% of asylum seekers were allowed to stay. They then become '**refugees**' and are able to stay for a set amount of time until their case is reviewed. As official refugees they can look for work. Much of the controversy over asylum seekers surrounds those who have been asked to leave – because many have 'disappeared' somewhere in the UK. There is a special group called the UK Border Agency who try to track them down (see Source I).

60,000 Asylum Seekers Lost Without Trace

At least 60,000 asylum seekers will be lost without trace as the UK Border Agency struggles to clear its backlog of claims, say MPs. They will be left in limbo as their claims are consigned to a growing pile of applications unlikely ever to be resolved, the Commons Home Affairs Select Committee says. The UK Border Agency has a backlog of up to 450,000 unresolved asylum cases. Some date back more than a decade.

SOURCE I: *From a Sky News Report, 11 January 2011.*

D) An illegal immigrant. These are people who enter Britain without permission (see Source J). They may be smuggled in with no documents at all, arrive with false documents, or overstay their visa (so the time they were allowed to stay has run out). Like asylum seekers, the whole topic of **illegal immigration** is very controversial. This is mainly because no-one, including the government, knows how many 'illegals' are in Britain. Some put the figure at 250,000, while an estimate in 2009 put the number as high as 1 million! The UK Border Agency works all over Britain (and in other countries where the illegal immigrants generally come from) to track down those people who do not have permission to be in Britain.

SOURCE J: *Britain's high-tech defence against people trying to gain illegal entry into the country. Here, an X-ray machine spots illegal immigrants smuggled in a lorry.*

WISE-UP Words

asylum seeker

economic migrant

illegal immigration

European Union

refugee

visa

Work

1 Imagine you've told someone at home (a parent, carer, brother or sister, for example) that you've just started the topic of immigration at school. In response, they asked you, 'Why are you studying immigration?'

In full sentences, write down what you would say in response to their question. Use the information on pages 6 and 7 (as well as the paragraphs at the top of page 8) to help you answer.

2 a What is the European Union?
  b What is the difference between an immigrant from an EU country and an immigrant from *outside* the EU?
  c Explain the difference between an asylum seeker and an illegal immigrant.

3 a Explain what is meant by the terms 'controversial' and 'divisive'.
  b Why do you think the topic of immigration has been labelled 'controversial' and 'divisive'?

MISSION ACCOMPLISHED?

• If a parent or carer asked why you are studying immigration, would you be able to give them good reasons?

Who were Britain's earliest immigrants?

_____ MISSION OBJECTIVES _____
- To find out when Britain's earliest immigrants arrived and understand why they came.
- To know what the lasting effects were on British life today.

We don't know much about the first people who lived in Britain. People didn't write anything down back then, so most of our information comes from fragments of bone, bits of stone, fossils, pottery and other artefacts. From these simple clues, experts have built up a basic picture of life in Britain thousands of years ago. But the picture isn't complete. There is still a lot we don't know. It's like an enormous jigsaw puzzle with most of the pieces missing!

The latest thinking is that for hundreds of thousands of years, there were probably no humans in Britain at all. But there were animals. These animals crossed over a 'land bridge' that linked what we now call the British Isles to mainland Europe.

Then, about half a million years ago, people from Europe began to arrive. These were Britain's earliest immigrants! They were **hunter-gatherers** who (as their name suggests) lived by gathering food (like nuts and fruit) and by killing animals for meat and furs. They moved around in small groups, sheltering in caves or building basic huts. They learned skills such as lighting fires and making sharp flint tools.

For many thousands of years, life in Britain remained largely unchanged. More hunter-gatherers would arrive from Europe and others would leave; some fought with other groups whilst others stayed isolated. Then, around 5,000 years ago, an important change happened. People learned how to farm. This meant that they began to produce their own food rather than having to hunt around for it. New settlers coming to Britain from Europe brought wheat and barley seeds to grow crops. They also brought animals to eat for meat, including pigs, sheep and goats, and they owned tame dogs too. They built more permanent homes and cleared large areas of woodland for farming.

SOURCE A: *An early settlement. The one-roomed huts were built of wood and mud with pieces of turf or straw thatch for roofs. Note the crops in the fields and the livestock fenced into pens. Most of the tools the people used were made from wood and stone rather than iron or other metals – which is why this period is usually known as the* **Stone Age!**

The Bronze Age

In about 2500 BC a new wave of settlers began arriving in Britain from central Europe. They were known as the **Beaker People** because of the decorated pottery cups they used (see Source B). The Beakers knew how to make things out of copper and gold. When tin was added to copper it made bronze… so the time of the Beaker people is often known as the **Bronze Age**. Soon tools and weapons made from metal replaced the ones made from stone and wood. The Beakers also introduced the first alcoholic drink to Britain (a kind of beer made from barley) and the wealthy women wore jewellery, pinned their hair up with decorated pins and wore woollen clothes instead of animal skins. The Beakers may even have been the first immigrants to tame wild horses for riding.

WISE-UP Words

hunter-gatherers

Stone Age

! FACT The land bridge

For thousands of years, hunter-gatherers could easily cross to Britain from Europe and back again because there was no English Channel. It was a period of Ice Age, so the sea was frozen solid. Then, around 8500 BC, the climate started to warm up and the ice began to melt. Over the next few thousand years, the land bridge gradually disappeared under water as the sea level rose… and Britain became an island.

↳ SOURCE B: *This beaker was part of a Stone Age burial site near Haddington, East Lothian.*
© *East Lothian Council*

After the Bronze Age

Over the next few thousand years, more and more different people arrived in Britain. Some came peacefully, whilst others were hostile invaders. Some came for only a short time but others settled for good. All of these immigrants left their mark on Britain. The cartoons on the next pages show some of these early immigrants.

THE CELTS

From central Europe

Began to settle in Britain around 500 BC

Lived in tribes that often fought brutally with each other

Farmers

Proud of their appearance – kept themselves clean using special soaps and perfumes

Wore shirts and cloaks that were colourfully dyed and embroidered

Built forts

Introduced bagpipes to Britain

Tribal business was done at yearly assemblies – land disputes settled, accused criminals tried and people appointed to important positions by vote

Celtic priests (druids) were in charge of religious rituals – some of their traditions survive today such as Halloween and May Day

THE ROMANS

Arrived 43 AD from Italy (Rome) and stayed for around 400 years

When the Roman army left, it is unclear how many stayed behind with their 'local' wives

Roman army made up of Gauls (from France), Germans and Hungarians – also evidence of a settlement of black Africans near York

Many of our main roads based on old Roman roads

Many Roman towns still important towns today – like Chester, York, Bath, Gloucester, Lincoln, Colchester and St Albans

Much of our language and some laws can be traced back to the Romans

Romans were the first in Britain to use calendars, coins, glass and bricks

Introduced cabbages, peas, wine, apples, grapes, turnips, carrots… and cats

THE ANGLO-SAXONS

Tribes of Angles and Saxons began arriving around 450 AD – after the Romans left

Invaded in small groups from Denmark and Northern Germany (other tribes also invaded around this time, such as the Jutes from Northern Germany)

Drove many of the Celtic tribes into Wales, Cornwall, Cumbria and Scotland

Before converting to Christianity they were pagans and worshipped many gods – some can be seen in our days of the week:
• Tiw (the god of combat) = Tuesday
• Woden (the god of war and wisdom) = Wodensday or Wednesday
• Thor (protector of mankind) = Thorsday or Thursday
• Freya (goddess of love and beauty) = Friday

Gave England its name – 'Angle-land', later England

Anglo-Saxon is one of the key 'base' languages of English – bed, cat, dog, tree, lick, jump, hunt, fox and fart are all words of Anglo-Saxon origin

Many of our counties and towns were created and named by them – if your town ends in 'ton', '-wich', '-worth', '-burn', '-hurst' or '-ham' then it was probably Anglo-Saxon originally

THE VIKINGS

Arrived after 800 AD from Denmark, Norway and Sweden

Like the Anglo-Saxons they were looking for land to settle on, but also for loot!

Some attacked and went home, others stayed

Took over much of north and east of Britain – places ending in '-by' and '-thorpe' were named by the Vikings

A man of Viking origin became King of England in 1016 (King Cnut)

THE NORMANS

Arrived from Normandy (France) after 1066

Rich Normans controlled England and Wales (but failed to take over Scotland and Ireland)

Built many fine castles, churches and cathedrals that still stand today

Over 10,000 words in our dictionaries come from these French settlers – e.g. royal, city, soldier, parliament and prince

Names like William, Stephen, Emma, Alice and Robert introduced by them

They invented surnames… and introduced playing chess and conkers

Also introduced deer, pheasants and rabbits… and planted the New Forest to hunt them in!

Introduced many new laws, traditions and customs still in use today

Changed the way the country was ruled and how people were taxed

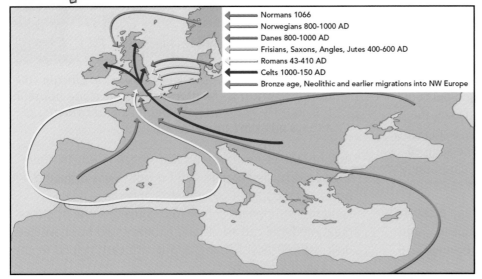

Normans 1066
Norwegians 800-1000 AD
Danes 800-1000 AD
Frisians, Saxons, Angles, Jutes 400-600 AD
Romans 43-410 AD
Celts 1000-150 AD
Bronze age, Neolithic and earlier migrations into NW Europe

⬑ SOURCE D: *Migration into Britain.*

WISE-UP Words

Beaker People

Bronze Age

hunter-gatherers

! FACT Rule Britannia

The Romans were the first people to use the name *Britannia* for Britain. The name was based on the word Pretannia – which is what the ancient Greeks used to call the British Isles, because they thought a Celtic tribe called the *Pretani* lived there. In fact the Pretani tribe lived mainly in Ireland – but the name Pretannia stuck, and later became Britannia, and then Britain!

Work

1 In your own words, explain the following terms:
  • The land bridge
  • The Stone Age
  • The Bronze Age

2 a Create a mind map with the title 'What did the earliest immigrants bring to Britain?' Each branch of your mind map should outline the contribution and impact of different groups of settlers – Celts, Romans, Anglo-Saxons, Vikings and Normans.
  b In your opinion, did some settlers contribute more than others? Explain your answer.

3 a How did 'Britain' get its name?
  b Britain has been described as 'made and remade by immigration'. Do you think this is an accurate description of Britain in the years up to 1066? Explain your answer carefully.

___MISSION ACCOMPLISHED?___

• Can you remember the lasting effects on Britain of **three** different groups of early immigrants?

JEWISH IMMIGRATION

People from all over the world with different beliefs, cultures, languages and traditions have been coming to Britain for thousands of years. Some came peacefully to start a new life; others invaded and came to conquer it. Some fled their own countries because of war, famine or **persecution**. And some were actually invited to come to Britain! This is why Jews first arrived… they were asked to come by King William (the Conqueror) after he won the Battle of Hastings in 1066. This Depth Study looks at the history of Jewish settlement in Britain. Why were the Jews asked here in the first place, and what was life like for them? And how have Jews continued to settle in Britain over the centuries?

1: The first Jewish community

_____ MISSION OBJECTIVES _____

- To find out *why* and *when* a group of Jews first came to England.
- To understand *how* they prospered over the next few hundred years.
- To know *why* and *when* they were expelled.

The Jews of 1066

A group of Jews from France was one of the first immigrant groups to come to Britain after 1066. At this time, Christians were banned from lending money to people in order to make a profit – but there were plenty of Christians who were eager to *borrow* money! Jews, however, were not banned from lending money so many of the first Jews to come to England became 'money-lenders'. They soon made fortunes because they charged a fee (called **interest**) to the people who borrowed from them. William the Conqueror invited the Jews to England because he thought they would be useful to him when it came to improving the nation!

The Jews help to change the nation

The first Jews who settled in Britain were banned from all businesses apart from money lending. But because the King had invited them over personally, it meant that they were protected by him. In fact, anyone found guilty of harming a Jew would be charged with damaging the King's property! Business was good as there were plenty of customers to lend money to, including the kings of England and Scotland, the Archbishop of Canterbury and hundreds of ordinary people.

Over the years, the Jews grew in numbers and prospered. More arrived from Italy, Spain, France and Russia… and a generation of Jews were born here and regarded themselves as English Jews!

⤷ SOURCE A: *"Aaron the Jew's House" in Lincoln still stands today. It is the oldest surviving stone house in the country. His money helped to build cathedrals, abbeys and nine monasteries.*

Around 200 years after Jews first settled in Britain, there were Jewish communities in 27 major towns including Bristol, Cambridge, Canterbury, Gloucester, Lincoln, London, Nottingham and Oxford. Indeed, some of our great medieval cathedrals and abbeys could not have been built without Jewish loans, and Jewish cash helped to pay for several royal armies.

Profit and pain

Despite their success in the money lending business, England's Jews faced much resentment and persecution. They were always seen as 'outsiders' because they weren't Christian like everyone else and they looked, spoke and dressed differently. Unlike most people in those days, many of them could read and write… and they were rich! People really didn't like having to pay their debts back to the Jewish money-lenders and on many occasions Jewish areas were attacked, despite their royal protection. Each time the angry mob would remember to burn or steal all the records of their debts! (See Source B.)

> 'In March 1190 a mix of soldiers, barons in debt to the Jews and those envious of Jewish wealth conspired to kill the Jews of York… 150 Jews fled to the Castle in York. The Jews had little rations and many killed themselves. On March 16th the castle was captured and those Jews left alive were murdered. The mob then stole the records of debts to Jews from a nearby Cathedral and burned them.'

↥ **SOURCE B:** *From www.jewishvirtualhistory.org, November 2010.*

Royal disapproval

Gradually the Jews in Britain began to lose their royal protection. Some kings fined or taxed the Jewish community so much that many Jews left Britain. During one ten-year period in the 1200s, the Jewish communities of England were fined and taxed a total of £420,000… that's over £220 million in today's money! One Jew – Abraham of Bristol – refused to pay one of the fines, so the king ordered that he have a tooth removed every day until he paid. Seven of his teeth were pulled out before Abraham gave in!

The Jew law

In 1272 royal protection for Jews in Britain came to an end. There were between 5,000 and 10,000 people who regarded themselves as Jews in Britain at this time, out of a population of around 3 million. Edward I passed a law that banned Jews from lending money. As they were also banned from doing any other job, many chose to leave the country. Those that remained had to wear a yellow patch of cloth on their clothes so people knew they were Jewish. Adolf Hitler forced Jews to do a similar thing hundreds of years later.

Soon after, Jews were banned from worshipping God in their own way – even in their own homes. Eventually, Edward I gave all Jews until 1 November 1290 to get out of the country – or face execution (see Source C). It would be 400 years before Jews came back to Britain!

> 'One of the boats paid to take Jews away struck a sandbar [a ridge of sand in the sea near the coast]. The captain told his passengers to get off the boat and stretch their legs. He then sailed away, shouting that the Jews should seek help from Moses. Maybe they tried. But no-one came to their aid. The sea did not part. They all drowned.'

↥ **SOURCE C:** *From* Bloody Foreigners *by Robert Winder, Abacus, 2004.*

WISE-UP Words

interest

persecution

Work

1 Explain why William the Conqueror brought the Jews to England.

2 **a** What do you think is meant by the term 'outsider'?
  b Why do you think Jews were seen as 'outsiders' in Medieval England?

3 Read Source B.
  a In your own words, explain what happened to the Jews of York.
  b Why do you think the 'records of debts' were burned by the angry mob?

4 **a** In the years immediately after 1066, in what way did the Jews receive royal protection?
  b Describe how that royal protection gradually came to an end in the years up to 1290.

5 **a** What is meant by the word 'tolerant'?
  b Was Medieval England tolerant towards Jews? Write a paragraph explaining your answer.

___ MISSION ACCOMPLISHED? ___

Could you explain in **four** sentences:
• why Jews came to England
• what they did and how they prospered
• how they were treated
• whether you think the Jews were a success here or not.

DEPTH STUDY

JEWISH IMMIGRATION

In 1290, King Edward I expelled all the Jews from England. It was over 350 years until England's leaders allowed Jews back in. There were only about 400 Jews living in England by 1690 and about 6000 by 1750. However, by 1850 the number of Jews had grown to about 40,000 (out of a population of 18 million). As their communities prospered, their contribution to British life grew. In fact, in 2006 Prime Minister Tony Blair said that 'it was impossible to imagine Britain without the Jews'. He went on to say that these immigrants and their descendants 'have made the country a better place', and that the values of British Jews today are 'the best of what Britain stands for'. So what did he mean? What is the Jewish story in Britain? And how have Jews made Britain 'a better place'?

2: The return of the Jews

MISSION OBJECTIVES

- To remember why thousands of Jews came to Britain in the 1800s… and how they contributed to the British way of life.

A success story?

In Victorian Britain the Jewish community had many success stories. By now, of course, many Jews regarded themselves as 'British'. The vast majority had been born in Britain, spoke English and lived typical British lifestyles. The first Jewish Mayor of London took office in 1855 and shortly afterwards Lionel de Rothschild became the first Jewish MP. Since then, the British Parliament has never been without Jewish politicians. In 1874 Benjamin Disraeli became Britain's first Jewish Prime Minister.

New Jews

In the 1870s and 1880s there was a new influx of Jews from Russia and Poland. Around 120,000 had arrived by 1914, fleeing religious attacks (called **pogroms**) in their own countries. Apart from their faith, these refugees had little in common with the Jews already living in Britain. They looked different, were largely uneducated and didn't speak any English. They worked hard but generally lived in the worst housing in the poorest areas. They were badly paid but were charged high rents for their overcrowded, disease-ridden rooms. And as more Jews arrived, anger and hostility towards them grew, mainly because they were accused of taking jobs from English workers. This is a familiar theme with any new immigrant group!

SOURCE A: *A photograph of Benjamin Disraeli, twice Prime Minister of Britain. He was born a Jew but converted to Christianity when he was a young man. He was also a talented writer of novels. When he died, Queen Victoria herself placed flowers on his grave!* ↵

SOURCE B: *An engraving of Wentworth Street, Whitechapel, a poor area of London, 1872. It shows not only poor Jews, but other immigrants – Irish, Indians and Germans, for example* ↱

Improving lives

There were three main kinds of work for the new Jewish immigrants – making clothes, shoemaking or furniture-making. This was mainly in small back-street workshops known as 'sweatshops' because of the warm conditions and long hours. But the Jews did very well in their new trades. Jewish communities soon gained a reputation as hardworking, law-abiding areas full of people with ambition and keen business sense. One immigrant called Michael Marks opened a market stall selling goods for a penny in 1894. His business partner was Tom Spencer, an Englishman. By 1900 Marks & Spencer had 36 outlets and it is now one of the best known high street stores in the world. Jack Cohen, the son of Polish Jewish immigrants, set up a business in Hackney in London selling (among other things) tea from a supplier called T.E. Stockwell. He soon created a brand name for his business by using part of his surname and the initials of his main supplier… and TESCO was born!

Our oldest ethnic minority

The Jewish community are now a successful and important part of British society. Jews live all over Britain but have particularly large communities in London, Manchester, Leeds and Glasgow. It was in 2006 during commemorations of 350 years since Jews were re-admitted into Britain that Prime Minister Tony Blair said that Jewish people were 'Britain's oldest ethnic minority' with a 'deep loyalty to our nation'. He went on to say that the Jewish communities of Britain have shown that 'it is possible to retain a clear faith and a clear identity and, at the same time, be thoroughly British'.

British Jews who today continue to excel in the world of business include Lord Alan Sugar, Philip Green (owner of TopShop, BHS and Dorothy Perkins), Bernard Lewis (owner of River Island) and Richard Desmond (a newspaper, magazine and TV station owner). Many British Jews have been successful in showbusiness too, including Elizabeth Taylor, Orlando Bloom and Joan Collins on the big screen and Matt Lucas and Sacha Baron Cohen in the world of comedy. Many Jews have fought for Britain too, including poet and soldier Siegfried Sassoon, and six British Jews have received the Victoria Cross, the highest award for bravery while serving their country.

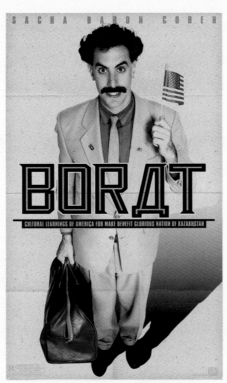

⌐ SOURCE C: *Sacha Baron Cohen is a British comedian, actor, and writer.*

! **FACT** Anti-Jewish feeling

A campaign to stop immigration began in the late 1800s. A number of key politicians supported it and in 1905 the first Aliens Act was passed by Parliament, limiting the number of Jewish immigrants.

Work

1 For what reasons did large numbers of Jews arrive in Britain in the 1870s and 1880s?
   b Describe how the 'new arrivals' were treated.
   c Can you think of reasons why the new Jewish immigrants were treated this way?

2 Look at Source B. Look closely at the picture. Firstly, describe what you see – and then try to explain what you think the artist thought about immigrants.

3 Do you agree with Prime Minister Tony Blair? Explain whether you think (like Tony Blair does) that Jewish people have made Britain 'a better place'.
   Give reasons for your answer.

MISSION ACCOMPLISHED?

• Can you recall why thousands of Jews came to Britain in the 1800s… and how several Jewish immigrants (or their descendants) contributed to the British way of life?

On 4 October 1936, in a poor area of the East End of London, women could be seen throwing bottles of urine at policemen. Children dropped marbles under the hooves of police horses and burst bags of pepper in front of their noses. People built barricades from paving stones, fence posts and overturned lorries. These people, mainly poor Jewish residents, were helped by dockworkers and trade-unionists. Their aim was to stop a political march through the streets of a Jewish area of London. The police became targets because they were there to clear a path through the streets for the marchers. This confrontation became known as the Battle of Cable Street. So what was the protest about? Why did the march go through a Jewish area? Why did the police get involved? And what has the Battle of Cable Street got to do with the story of immigration?

3: The Battle of Cable Street

MISSION OBJECTIVES

- To explain what the 'Battle of Cable Street' was… and why it is a significant event in the history of Jewish immigration to Britain.

Britain's Nazis?

The British Union of Fascists (BUF) was a 1930s British political party with many views similar to those of Adolf Hitler's Nazi Party in Germany. Its leader was a man named Oswald Mosley. He had grown popular in the early 1930s because of his views on – amongst other things – immigration. During this time many people in Britain were without jobs and Mosley became well-known for his ideas on limiting immigration. He argued that immigrants took the jobs of English workers. He claimed that 'England should be for the English' and, like many others before him, directed his hatred towards the Jewish communities. By 1934 the BUF had around 40,000 members, and at meetings they gave the Nazi salute and chanted 'Hail Mosley!' and 'Down with Jews!' (see Sources A and B).

Political marches

It was common for the BUF to go on marches through city centres. These were always followed by a speech by Mosley. Marches were a way of showing the party's strength and organization, as well as a chance to get their message across to a wider audience.

On Sunday 4 October 1936, Mosley planned to send thousands of his supporters into the East End of London dressed in uniforms that mimicked those of Hitler's Nazis. The area was full of poor workers – and had a large Jewish community.

↵ SOURCE A: Oswald Mosley, leader of the BUF. Note the supporters giving the infamous "Nazi salute".

↰ SOURCE B: The BUF has its own newspaper. Note how the news headline describes Jews as "Aliens"!

The Battle of Cable Street

When news got out of the BUF's march, a crowd of up to a quarter of a million people gathered to block the route. The police arrived too, and tried to clear a way for the BUF. At the time, political marches like this were legal, and so the police were doing their job of ensuring the rights of a political group to march freely. But the crowd had other ideas!

At around 3pm the Fascists reached Cable Street… and were stopped! They waited for the police to clear a path through the crowd, but it was impossible. Soon the police and some members of the crowd clashed. Barricades of old mattresses, a broken-down lorry and broken paving stones appeared. The police were bombarded with missiles from the crowd and banners appeared that read 'They shall not pass' (see Sources C and D).

> 'We were all side by side. I was moved to tears to see bearded Jews and Irish dockers standing up to Mosley. I shall never forget that as long as I live, how working class people could get together to oppose the evil of racism.'

SOURCE C: *Eyewitness Bill Fishman, quoted in the Guardian newspaper online, 30 September 2006, by Audrey Gillan.*

After an unsuccessful hour or so, the police left and the BUF marched *around* the Jewish area and headed for the centre of London. They put up posters saying 'Kill the dirty Jews' and smashed Jewish shop windows as they went.

SOURCE D: *A photograph taken during the Battle of Cable Street.*

The aftermath

Shortly after the Battle of Cable Street, the government gave the police the right to ban political marches like the one that took place in the East End that day (see Source E). Soon support for Mosley died down. In 1940, after the outbreak of World War Two when Britain was at war with Hitler, the BUF was disbanded and Mosley was **interned**.

Work

1 **a** Who were the BUF?
   b Why do you think the BUF chose the East End of London for their march on 4 October 1936?

2 **a** Why did the police become targets of violence during the Battle of Cable Street?
   b What is your opinion regarding the violence against the police on that day?

3 The BUF were prevented from marching down Cable Street but still marched into the centre of London, smashed Jewish shop windows and put up nasty posters. Who, in your opinion, won the Battle of Cable Street?

4 Read Source E.
   What do you think the writer means when he says that the Battle of Cable Street was an 'important emblem for the acceptance of immigrants'?

> 'The Battle of Cable Street is an important emblem for the acceptance of immigrants.'

SOURCE E: *From* Bloody Foreigners *by Robert Winder, Abacus, 2004.*

MISSION ACCOMPLISHED?

- Why do you think the events of 4 October 1936 are regarded by historians as so important in the history of Jewish immigration?

19

Why do people come to Britain?

MISSION OBJECTIVES

- To be able to explain what is meant by the terms 'voluntary migration' and 'forced migration'.

Many of the first people to come to Britain came as invaders. While lots of these invaders simply returned home to their own lands with their plunder, others (like various tribes of Angles, Saxons, Celts, Vikings and so on) became settlers and made Britain their home.

Types of migration

The movement of people from one place to another is called **migration** – and a person who moves is known as a **migrant**. People who move into a country are called immigrants, while those who move out of a country are known as **emigrants**. People, or groups of people, have always moved between different countries all over the world. Some move because they want to, while others move because they have no choice and are forced to. Generally speaking we can put this migration into two categories – *forced* and *voluntary*.

Voluntary migration is when people *choose* to move. For example:

- They might want to improve their chances of finding a job… or a better-paid job.
- They might want to improve their quality of life – by living or working in a better environment or by moving to a country where there are better services such as healthcare or transport.
- They may be encouraged to move by the government or the king or queen of another country – perhaps they are skilled tradesmen who are invited to set up a business in a different country, or they are filling job vacancies in vital industries.

! FACT Not just one-way traffic
People don't just come to live in Britain… they leave Britain too! People emigrate for all sorts of reasons – including a better job, a better climate or more opportunities. Most people will know someone who has emigrated to another country, perhaps to retire or because they have a job offer. In 2009, for example, 518,000 people came to settle in Britain… and 317,000 people left.

Forced migration is when people have little or *no choice* but to move. For example:

- They may have to leave their homeland because of natural disasters such as floods or earthquakes.
- They might belong to a group, race or religion that is being persecuted in their own country and are afraid that they will be killed if they stay there.
- They may be fleeing from dangers such as war or famine.
- They may be brought to a country against their will – as slaves or servants for example.

Over the centuries many thousands of people of all sorts of races and religions have come to Britain from many different countries. For some it was voluntary migration – but for others it was forced migration. Look through the following characters carefully and try to work out which people chose to move here and which had little or no choice.

In the 1600s and 1700s thousands of French Protestants came to Britain. They were known as **Huguenots** and were fleeing attacks by French Catholics. Many were successful businessmen who brought new skills and techniques over to Britain. These included improved methods of making glass, watches, clocks, spectacles, hats, wigs, silk and fine paper (which made the printing of paper money possible). They even set up their own charity organizations (called Friendly Societies) to help those amongst them who had fallen on hard times, an idea that was copied by English workers years later. In fact, some historians have said that the arrival of the Huguenots was one of the key reasons that Britain developed from a farming nation to a world-leading industrial nation in the 1800s.

WISE-UP Words

emigrants

Huguenots

migrant

migration

Many generations of Irish people have come to Britain. In the 1840s, for example, thousands emigrated to Britain because of famine. Lots of them found jobs building Britain's canals, roads and railways. There were further surges of Irish immigration in the 1930s, 1950s and 1960s, mostly people looking for work in Britain's expanding cities. In fact, according to the 2001 Census, 6 million people (10% of the total British population) had Irish parents or grandparents. The Irish, therefore, have made a huge impact on Britain – and many famous Brits like Ant and Dec, Paul McCartney, Tony Blair and Wayne Rooney have strong Irish roots.

Jewish people have settled in Britain for many hundreds of years. First asked over by William the Conqueror in 1066, they prospered as money-lenders, goldsmiths and doctors. Loans from Jews helped the Church build some of Britain's finest cathedrals and helped Kings to pay for royal armies. Jews were expelled from Britain in 1290 but were allowed to return in the 1600s. Since then the Jewish community has again prospered, particularly in areas like banking, business, clothing, science, medicine, literature, TV and film.

Immigrants from Eastern European countries (like Poland, Hungary, Romania and the Czech Republic) have been settling in Britain for years. In the 1940s and 1950s, many came to escape wars and persecution in their homelands. Thousands helped Britain fight in World War Two. In recent years many Eastern European countries have become part of the European Union, so its citizens have the right to come and live and work in Britain (in exactly the same way that any British person can go and work in any EU country).

People of West Indian and African descent have lived in Britain for hundreds of years. Some were brought here as slaves or servants when Britain was involved in the slave trade in the seventeenth and eighteenth centuries. Then, in the 1950s, another wave of West Indians came over. They were encouraged to come by the British government because Britain had a serious shortage of workers after World War Two.

Chinese immigrants first came to Britain to work over 150 years ago, but it was in the 1950s and 1960s that their numbers really grew. Most were from British-controlled areas like Hong Kong, Malaysia and Singapore. Many were looking for jobs and set up businesses like laundries, grocery shops and restaurants. The first Chinese restaurant in Britain opened in London in 1908 – and now there are over 14,000 Chinese restaurants and takeaways, making over £1.7 billion a year! Today there are around 400,000 British Chinese people – and every year British Chinese students perform best in school.

Many immigrants from India, Pakistan and Bangladesh (South Asia) came to Britain in the 1950s and 1960s looking for work and better education opportunities. Many started their own small businesses or worked in industries like textiles or steel making. Today around 4 million people of South Asian descent live in Britain.

Around 70,000 Kenyan and Ugandan Asians moved to Britain from their homes in Africa in the 1960s and 1970s. They came here in order to escape racist attitudes and intolerance in Africa at the time. In Uganda, for example, the President Idi Amin told Ugandan Asians to leave the country after he claimed he'd had a dream in which God told him to expel them!

Work

1 Write a sentence or two about the following key words:
   • Migration
   • Migrant
   • Immigrant
   • Emigrant

2 What is the difference between voluntary migration and forced migration? Make sure you use examples when answering this question.

3 Over the last four pages you have looked at several immigrant groups who have settled in Britain over the last 1,000 years – Jews, Huguenots, Irish, Eastern Europeans, people of West Indian and African descent, Chinese, South Asians and Kenyan and Ugandan Asians.

   Create a timeline showing when these different people and cultures came to Britain. When labelling your timeline, try to include details of the reasons they came to Britain (was it voluntary or forced migration, for example?) and one or two sentences saying what changes they brought about and/or what contributions they made to the British way of life.

Top Tip: This task is ideally suited to be done on A3 paper – and made bright and colourful for use as a class display!

MISSION ACCOMPLISHED?

• Can you explain the difference between 'forced migration' and 'voluntary migration'... and give several examples of each?

BLACK IMMIGRATION

There are many different reasons why black people have come to Britain over the centuries. Some black settlers came to seek a better life, perhaps escaping poverty or fleeing from war zones. Others were invited by the British king or government because they had particular skills that were in short supply in Britain at the time. Some were brought here against their will as slaves or servants. This Depth Study looks at the history of black immigration into Britain. It charts why black people first arrived, how they settled through the ages, why there was a sudden influx in the 20th century, and how Britain's black population has made such a positive contribution to the country.

1: Britain's first black immigrants

MISSION OBJECTIVES
- To establish why black people first came to Britain and how they were treated.
- To understand how several extraordinary black Britons made a dramatic impact on British culture and society.

Look at Source A. It is an extract from a 20-metre-long picture made to celebrate the birth of one of King Henry VIII's children. The full picture shows the king himself surrounded by dozens of servants, officials, nobles, soldiers, visitors, and six musicians on horseback playing trumpets. And one of them is black! His name was John Blanke and he was paid 20 shillings a month by the King (around £450 in today's money). So how common were skilled black immigrants like John Blanke in Tudor England? How did black immigrants get to England in the first place? And what has life been like over the centuries for some of the first black Brits?

↵ **SOURCE A:** *John Blanke worked for two Tudor kings – Henry VII and Henry VIII. Little is known about how he got to Britain but it is assumed he was brought here as a slave. His name is actually a (very poor) Tudor joke – 'blanke' means white!*

Britain's black emporer

The first black people to come to Britain were probably black Roman soldiers. Certainly by 200 AD there were many black Roman officers, soldiers and slaves based in Britain. In fact, Emperor Septimus Severus, who ruled the Roman Empire for 18 years, was black. And he lived in Britain for three years before his death, helping defend this part of his empire from invading tribes. He died in York of **pneumonia** in 211 AD.

Tudor times

There are some records of black people in Britain in the Middle Ages... but not many. However, by Tudor times there were large numbers of black Africans in Britain. Some may have come as sailors or perhaps traders, but most often they were slaves for rich merchants and nobles. Some, however, had specialized skills like John Blanke (see Source A). Another skilled black man was employed as a diver by King Henry VIII to search for the wreck of his favourite ship – the *Mary Rose* – in 1545. Sadly, we don't know what his name was.

By the reign of Henry VIII's daughter, Queen Elizabeth, there were several thousand black immigrants in Britain. And the Queen didn't like this. In fact, she wrote to the mayors of major towns complaining of 'too manie blacks' in England and asked that 'those kinde of people should be sente forth of the land'. Her requests were ignored though!

The slavery years

Throughout the 17th and 18th centuries, Britain was heavily involved in the slave trade. British merchants made millions of pounds buying and selling black African men, women and children to farmers in the West Indies and North and South America. British ships transported the slaves over the Atlantic Ocean – and then brought back the sugar, cotton, spices, rum and tobacco that the slaves farmed and sold it all over Britain and Europe. It has been estimated that the profits made by British slave traders on the 2,500,000 Africans bought and sold between 1630 and 1807 was around £12 million… which would be equal to around £1 billion today! This money helped Britain become one of the richest and most powerful nations in the world.

Some of the black Africans ended up in Britain. They came as slaves belonging to ships' captains or as servants to rich people (see Source B). Some arrived as stowaways. It was even viewed as quite fashionable for a rich family to have a black slave at this time. In some paintings they are shown grouped with the family's pets or horses, a sign of their status in the house! By 1800 the black population in London was estimated at around 20,000 people.

WISE-UP Words

pneumonia

Life in Britain

Most black people who were brought here as slaves lived and died as servants. If they managed to escape (by running away or being released into freedom) they generally lived in poverty. They usually headed to London and lived in the poor East End area. Many were forced to turn to begging, prostitution or pick-pocketing. And often they became targets of the most severe racism. In 1788, for example, author Philip Thicknesse wrote that 'London is full of these black men… in almost every village, mischievous as monkeys and infinitely more dangerous'.

SOURCE C: *Part of a painting entitled 'Captain Graham in his cabin' by Hogarth. Music was one area in which black people could get a job if they managed to gain their freedom. Many served as drummers in the army or navy, or as street entertainers.* ↱

Amazing achievements

Some black servants grew to be liked and respected by their masters and managed to go on to better things. Dr Johnson (who wrote the first ever English dictionary) refused to let his black, Jamaican-born servant Francis Barber go and buy food for his cat, saying that 'it wasn't good to employ human beings to work for animals'.

↰ SOURCE E: *A painting of Ottobah Cugoano who, like Equiano, was a freed slave and wrote a powerful book that destroyed many of the old arguments in defence of slavery. The two men even formed a pressure group – the Sons of Africa – with other leading members of London's black community to fight for the abolition of slavery.*

Johnson also enrolled Barber in school and left him £70 a year and a gold watch in his will! Barber himself married a white Englishwoman, had four children and opened a shop selling cloth. His descendants still live in Staffordshire today. Ignatius Sancho, a servant of the Duke of Montagu, managed to buy his freedom and set up a very fashionable shop in London where the rich and famous would go to buy sugar, drink tea and talk politics. And as a money-earning home-owner in Westminster, he qualified to vote in the elections of 1774 and 1780. He is the first black person to have voted in Britain!

Other black Britons achieved amazing things too, notably in the fight to end slavery. Olaudah Equiano (a former slave who managed to buy his freedom) moved to Britain where he married and wrote his life story. His book was a best-seller and turned many people against slavery. The fact that he was clearly intelligent and articulate made nonsense of the claims at the time that black people were inferior and only good for manual work or playing musical instruments!

The 19th century and beyond

In the 1800s, Britain's black community continued to make extraordinary and far-reaching contributions to society…

**Mary Seacole
(1805–1881)**

The daughter of a black Jamaican, Nurse Seacole used her own money to go and provide medical help for British soldiers in the Crimean War.

**George Bridgtower
(1780–1860)**

The son of a black West Indian, he was a brilliant violinist, making his professional debut at the age of nine. He moved to London aged 11 to work as a musician for the Prince of Wales. He was a close friend of Beethoven.

**William Cuffay
(1788–1870)**

The son of a slave, Cuffay was a crucial figure in the campaign to gain the vote for working men.

**Samuel Coleridge-Taylor
(1875–1912)**

The son of an African father and an English mother, Coleridge-Taylor was a brilliant composer and campaigner for civil rights.

SOURCE D: *Walter Tull was the 2nd black man to play at the top level of English football, he appears in a photo with the rest of the Tottenham Hotspurs Team on page 7. He was also the first black officer in the British Army to command white soldiers. Here he is pictured in his army uniform.*

Work

1 a Write a sentence or two about:
  - John Blanke
  - Emperor Septimus Severus
  - Francis Barber
  - Ignatius Sancho

b What sort of people do you think these men were? Explain what you think they were like as individuals, using words to describe what sort of characters and personalities you think they had.

2 What was Queen Elizabeth's attitude towards black immigration in Tudor England?

3 a In what ways did the slave trade increase the amount of black people in Britain? Explain your answer carefully.

b What part did Olaudah Equiano and Ottobah Cugoano play in the story of the slave trade?

4 Describe the typical black immigrant experience in eighteenth and early nineteenth century Britain.

5 Bridgtower, Cuffay, Seacole, Coleridge-Taylor and Tull regularly appear on lists of 'Great Black Britons'. Why do you think they each appear on the list?

Walter Tull (1888–1918)

The grandson of a slave, Tull became one of Britain's first black professional footballers, playing for Tottenham Hotspur and Northampton Town. During World War One he was in the Footballers' Battalion of the Middlesex Regiment and fought in the Battle of the Somme in 1916. He was the first black officer in the British Army to command white soldiers – but he was killed in action in March 1918 aged 29.

—— MISSION ACCOMPLISHED? ——

- Can you name **five** extraordinary black Britons… and outline their significant contributions to the British way of life?

On 22 June 1948 a ship named Empire Windrush arrived at Tilbury docks in London. On board were 492 people – most of them men – who had come to live in Britain. It was an event that would change the face of British society forever. So just what made these newcomers special, and why were they moving to Britain in the first place? How were they, and others who followed in later years, treated? And how did they help to change life in Britain?

2: The Windrush Generation

MISSION OBJECTIVES

- To find out some reasons why the Windrush immigrants came to Britain… and establish what life was like for many of them when they got here.

Moving to the 'mother country'

In 1948 Britain still had an Empire, a collection of nations around the world that Britain controlled. During World War Two people from all over the British Empire helped Britain win the war. At this time, many islands in the Caribbean Sea (known as the West Indies) were part of the British Empire, including Jamaica, Barbados and Trinidad. These islands had supplied over 10,000 men for Britain's army, navy and airforce – and they had been proud of their role in helping Britain (see Source B). However, soon after the fighting ended, they found they had little to celebrate upon returning home. Life was very hard in the Caribbean in the 1940s. Jamaica had been devastated by a hurricane in 1944, there was no tourist industry and the price of sugar – the Caribbean's main export – was at an all-time low. To ambitious men seeking better opportunities, it was clear that their future lay abroad – under the grey skies of Britain… the 'mother country'!

↖ SOURCE A: *The first black immigrants to arrive in Britain from the West Indies after World War Two became known as the 'Windrush generation'.*

↵ SOURCE B: *West Indian troops fought for Britain during the Second World War. The photograph shows members of a Trinidad unit of the South Caribbean Force being trained in jungle fighting.*

'What were they thinking, these 492 men from Jamaica and Trinidad, as the *Empire Windrush* slid upstream? Standing by the rail this morning, high above the landing-stage at Tilbury, one of them looked over the unlovely town to the grey-green fields beyond and said, "If this is England I like it". May he and his friends suffer no sharp disappointment.

It was curiously touching to see against the white walls of the ship row upon row of dark, thoughtful faces looking down upon England, most of them for the first time. Had they thought England a golden land in a golden age?

What manner of men are these the Empire Windrush has brought to Britain? This morning, on the decks, I spoke with the following: a builder, a carpenter, an apprentice accountant, a farm worker, a tailor, a welder, a spray-painter, a boxer, a musician, a mechanic, a valet, a calypso singer, and a law student. Or thus they described themselves.

And what had made them leave Jamaica? In most case, lack of work. Many can earn no wages. One man has been idle two years. Most of the married men have left their wives and children at home, and hope to send for them later. Only five complete families sailed.

They are, then, as mixed a collection of humanity as one might find. Some will be good workers, some bad. Many are "serious-minded persons" anxious to succeed. No doubt the singers will find audiences somewhere. So will the dance-band which is journeying to Liverpool at this moment. And the boxer, who is going to meet his manager at Birkenhead, will surely find fights in plenty. Not all intend to settle in Britain; a 40-year-old tailor, for example, hopes to stay here for a year, and then go on and make his home in Africa.

But the more world-wise among them are conscious of the deeper problem posed. In the past Britain has welcomed displaced persons who cannot go home. "This is right," said one of the immigrants. "Surely then, there is nothing against our coming, for we are British subjects. If there is – is it because we are coloured?"'

WISE-UP Words

British Nationality Act

Commonwealth

↵ SOURCE C: *From an article in the Guardian newspaper, 23 June 1948.*

Why Britain?

In 1948 Parliament passed the **British Nationality Act**. This meant that all the people of the Empire – now called the **Commonwealth** – were British passport holders and were allowed to live and work in Britain. So even if you had never been to Britain before, as a British citizen you had the right to enter the country and work and settle there if you wanted to. Many West Indians saw this as a great opportunity. Having been brought up speaking English, named after British heroes and educated to believe in Queen and country, many West Indians felt very 'British'. And at the time Britain was very short of workers to help run the transport system, postal service and hospitals.

↰ SOURCE D: *A photograph of three prize-winning nurses from a London hospital in 1954. One was from England, one from Trinidad and the other from Jamaica. The NHS, London Transport, the British Hotels Association and the British Transport Commission all encouraged people from the Caribbean to move to Britain. By 1958 there were approximately 8000 West Indians working on Britain's public transport system, for example.*

Welcome Windrush?

The voyage of the Windrush made headlines in Britain before the ship had even arrived. Thousands of immigrants from Europe had been pouring into the country ever since the war finished, but it was the arrival of this one ship of English-speaking, Christian, British citizens that made the headlines. Newspapers were full of stories of the 'colour problem' that was heading towards British shores and some politicians demanded that the ship should be turned around and sent back. When Windrush finally docked, the smartly dressed West Indians smiled nervously at the journalists and one of them sang a song called 'London's the Place for Me'. Soon, they had all found jobs – and their friends and relatives followed in search of work.

'The second day in England I was offered five jobs. If someone want to leave, let them leave, but I have been here during the War fighting Nazi Germany and I came back and help build Britain. People said that we would not stay longer than one year; we are here, and I and my people are here to stay.'

↳ SOURCE E: *Sam King – one of the passengers on the* Empire Windrush.

The British experience

Not all white Britons welcomed Britain's newest citizens. Many West Indians found that the colour of their skin provoked hostile reactions. Some immigrants found good jobs, but many – whatever their qualifications – ended up working in low-paid jobs as cleaners, ticket collectors and hospital porters. They also experienced difficulties finding decent places to live. For many on low incomes, who needed to find housing close to work, the only places they could find were in the most run-down areas of town. And often they would be faced with openly racist signs put up in the windows of landlords looking for renters specifying 'No Irish, No Blacks, No dogs'. This prejudice led to 'black areas' being created in some of Britain's major cities.

↵ SOURCE F: *Some of the men from the Windrush, dressed in their best suits, photographed upon their arrival in London on 22 June 1948. These famous pictures have come to symbolize the beginning of Britain's modern multicultural society.*

Violence and riots

On occasions there were outbreaks of violence in areas where large numbers of West Indians lived. In 1958, in Nottingham and in Notting Hill, London, there were several weeks of violence when white youths attacked black youths on the streets, at nightclubs, and in their homes. In fact, the Notting Hill Carnival (which now attracts over one million visitors each year) began as a gesture of defiance by the black community against the widespread racial attacks of the time.

! FACT Numbers

In the 1940s, Caribbean arrivals in Britain numbered around 500 to 700 a year. By 1953 that had gone up to around 2,200 a year. By 1960 there were around 40,000 immigrants arriving from the West Indies each year. This outnumbered all other immigrants from all other areas of the world. The newcomers mainly settled in industrial areas such as Liverpool, Manchester, Birmingham, Bristol, Nottingham, Leeds, Bradford, Leicester, Walsall, Wolverhampton and Luton. Most, however, stayed in London.

⤶ SOURCE G: *During the 1950s and 1960s, lots of racial tension was caused by 'mixed' relationships, usually between black men and white women. In fact, surveys at the time showed that two-thirds of Britons were against mixed marriages. This photograph shows a couple who lived through the prejudice of that time. Jamaican-born immigrant Siebert Mattison (a steel worker) is pictured in 1955 with his Welsh wife and two little children in their one-roomed Birmingham home.*

Yet despite the discrimination, the racial tension and obstacles such as low pay and poor housing, thousands and thousands of West Indians decided to make Britain their home. Some did go back to the West Indies but most remained, determined to stay despite the difficulties they faced. And the contribution they have made to British society and culture is huge.

Work

1 a List reasons why many people wanted to leave the Caribbean at the end of World War Two.
  b List reasons why people from the Caribbean may have chosen to come to Britain.

2 Look at Source B
  a What was the *Empire Windrush*?
  b List at least ten different jobs that the passengers on the ship claimed they could do.
  c Find at least two reasons contained in the article that explain why some of the passengers on the ship came to Britain.
  d According to the writer of the article, which passengers on board does he think will definitely find work?

3 Use all the information and sources on pages 30 and 31 to answer the following question: Who were the 'Windrush generation' and what was life like for them in 1940s and 1950s Britain?

4 a What is meant by the word 'tolerant'?
  b Do you think Britain in the 1940s and 1950s was a tolerant place? Explain your answer carefully.

—— **MISSION ACCOMPLISHED?** ——

• Can you write an explanation of the term 'Windrush generation'?

In 1968 a politician named Enoch Powell made a famous speech about immigration (see Source A). He said that white people were becoming 'strangers in their own country' and could soon expect 'the black man to have the whip hand over the white man'. He predicted that Britain's rivers would be 'foaming with much blood' if so many immigrants kept coming into Britain and were given equal rights with whites. Powell was sacked for making the speech – but surveys showed that around three-quarters of British people agreed with him! So why did Powell make his comments? How did the British public respond? Was the number of immigrants really increasing dramatically at the time – or did the government limit it? And how has the British government tried to prevent or reduce racial conflict in Britain?

3: Rivers of blood

MISSION OBJECTIVES

- To understand the circumstances in which the 'rivers of blood' speech was made.
- To understand how the British government tried to prevent or reduce racial tension and conflict in the 1960s and 1970s.

↵ **SOURCE A:** *On Saturday 20 April 1968 Enoch Powell made a controversial speech in Birmingham, in which he warned his audience of what he believed would be the consequences of continued unchecked immigration from the Commonwealth to Britain.*

↳ **SOURCE B:** *Graffiti in London, 1968. Clearly Enoch Powell had many supporters for his views on immigration.*

Hard work and restrictions

Throughout the 1950s and 1960s, immigration to Britain increased. West Indians were the biggest group of immigrants, but thousands of Indians and Pakistanis also arrived. Many Chinese immigrants came too, as well as Sikhs from the Punjab. The vast majority worked incredibly hard and for long hours. The stereotype about Pakistani shops being 'open all hours' began at this time, mainly because it was true – Pakistani shop owners worked unsocial hours to supply local people at any time of day. By 1970 there were about 1,000 Indian restaurants and nearly 4,000 Chinese takeaways in Britain. However, the familiar complaints about 'foreigners' taking jobs from white British people were soon common. And riots like those in Nottingham and London in 1958 scared the government into action.

New rules

In 1962 the government passed the **Commonwealth Immigrants Act**, which said that people could only enter Britain from Commonwealth countries if they were skilled professionals who had been given permission to work here. Before this, anyone from any country in the Commonwealth (the former British Empire), like India, Pakistan, Jamaica, etc., could come and live in Britain without restriction. This new law changed all that!

But for some people this new limit on immigration was not enough. In 1964 a Conservative candidate stood for election to Parliament in Smethwick, West Midlands with the slogan 'If you want a nigger for a neighbour – vote Labour'. And won! And in 1967, a new group formed with the slogan 'Britain for the British'. They were called the **National Front** and by 1970 they had over 10,000 members.

Government action

It would be wrong to think that the government at the time did nothing to address racial discrimination in Britain. In 1965, for example, the **Race Relations Act** became the first law to directly address racism. It made discrimination illegal on the grounds of 'colour, race or ethnic or national origins'. It also set up the **Race Relations Board** to promote good racial relations. However, the Act only applied in 'public places' like hotels and restaurants and didn't cover housing, employment or financial things such as mortgages and car insurance.

A few years later, in 1968, the government further tightened up the law on immigrants entering Britain. A new **Commonwealth Immigration Act** meant that they had to show a 'close connection' with the UK. At the same time, the government introduced a new **Race Relations Act (1968)**. This made it illegal to refuse housing or employment to people because of their colour. And it was at this time that Enoch Powell made his infamous 'rivers of blood' speech, predicting racial conflict if the government allowed the current levels of immigration to continue.

Reaction to Powell's speech

Powell was sacked for what he said and many leading politicians publically criticized him. *The Times* declared that it was 'an evil speech'. But Powell also had many supporters. Some politicians argued that he had a right to voice his opinions, and 1,000 dockworkers in London went on strike in protest at his sacking. They marched towards Downing Street carrying banners reading 'Don't Knock Enoch' and 'Back Britain, not Black Britain'. Groups supporting Powell's views, like the National Front, became more popular too. By 1974 they had around 20,000 members and went on huge marches through city centres. They even put forward candidates for local and national elections.

More laws

The government continued to tighten up immigration in the 1970s. **The Immigration Act of 1971** severely restricted immigration from the Commonwealth, unless immigrants had a parent or grandparent born in Britain. However, the government promised to be 'tough but fair' on immigrants, and in 1976 introduced a new, tougher Race Relations Act to protect immigrants' rights. This Act outlawed all discrimination in employment, housing, education, provision of goods and services, and much more. The Act also set up the **Commission for Racial Equality** to make sure the new laws were followed.

↳ **SOURCE C:** *Workers from Smithfield Meat Market in London marching through the city in protest about immigration, 1972.*

Work

1 Who was Enoch Powell, and why did he become so well known in 1968?

2 Look at Sources B and C. Each source features Enoch Powell in some way. Why do you think Enoch Powell had so much support in the late 1960s and early 1970s?

3 **a** Find three examples from these pages that could be used to support the claim that Britain should be ashamed of its treatment of and attitudes towards immigrants during the 1960s and 1970s.

 b Find three examples from these pages that could be used to support the claim that Britain responded in a positive way to the increase in immigration at this time.

___ **MISSION ACCOMPLISHED?** ___

- Can you describe and explain the following: 'rivers of blood' speech; Race Relations Act; Immigration Acts; National Front?

DEPTH STUDY
BLACK IMMIGRATION

Between 1945 and 1955, over a quarter of a million West Indians (the majority from Jamaica) settled in Britain. They helped the British economy recover after the war by taking jobs where there was a shortage of workers, like in hospitals, on the railways and with London Transport. But West Indians were not the only black immigrants to Britain. In time, they were followed by thousands more from ex-British Empire countries like Nigeria, Ghana, Uganda and Kenya.

4: Best of British

_____ MISSION OBJECTIVES _____

- To understand what is meant by the term 'black British'.
- To know how at least three black Britons have made a positive contribution to British society.

Over time, these immigrants began to settle down and start families. Their children (who had been born in Britain) regarded themselves not as immigrants (because they weren't!) but as 'black British'. By the 1970s a whole generation of young black Brits – with African and Caribbean heritage – had emerged. Today the black British population is around 1.4 million people (out of 60 million). And despite the difficulties faced by a lot of black Britons over the years, many have made a valuable and significant contribution to British life.

↵ SOURCE A: *Viv Anderson (the son of West Indian immigrants) became the first black player to represent England at football in a full international match in 1978. As a young player he endured racist abuse such as fans throwing fruit on the pitch. His manager, Brian Clough, responded by telling him to go back out and to "fetch me two pears and a banana".*

↰ SOURCE B: *Michael Fuller (son of Jamaican immigrants who came to Britain in the 1950s) was the first black Chief Constable in the UK.*

SOURCE C: *Sir Trevor McDonald (born in Trinidad) is one of Britain's most respected newsreaders and reporters. He was the first black newsreader in the UK and has won more awards than any other reporter.* ↱

SOURCE D: *Dame Kelly Holmes (her father was born in Jamaica, her mother is English) is a double Olympic Gold Medallist. Other prominent black or mixed race sportsmen include Lennox Lewis (former World undisputed Heavyweight Boxing Champion), Lewis Hamilton (Formula 1 World Champion), Daley Thompson (double Olympic Champion – Decathlon), Linford Christie (Olympic and World 100m Champion) and Christine Ohurougu (World, Olympic and Commonwealth 400m Champion).*

SOURCE F: *Diane Abbott (daughter of Jamaican immigrants) was Britain's first black female MP. She was first elected to Parliament in 1987, along with Bernie Grant (born in Guyana) and Paul Boateng (mixed Ghanaian and Scottish heritage).*

SOURCE E: *Johnson Beharry, born in Grenada, West Indies, became the first man to win the Victoria Cross (Britain's top bravery medal) since 1982 for services to his country in Iraq in 2004. When he received the medal from the Queen she said 'It's been rather a long time since I awarded one of these'.*

Work

1 Write a detailed explanation of the term 'black British'.

2 Look at Source A.
   a Why did Viv Anderson's manager send him out to the football pitch to pick up fruit?
   b What do you think of his manager's approach to this incident?

3 a Make a list of all the people mentioned on this page you knew about (or had heard of) before studying them on these pages.
   b Can you suggest any reasons why you knew about some of them, but not others?
   c Suggest other famous 'black Brits' who you think should feature on this page. Explain why you've chosen them.

4 Read the Fact box on Equality.
   a What is meant by the term 'equality'?
   b Why do you think the fact that black men are almost eight times more likely to be stopped by the police than white men is such a controversial statistic?

! FACT Equality

Britain's black communities continue to face problems even now. For reasons that are still the subject of fierce controversy, a survey in 2006 showed that black pupils were three times more likely to be excluded from school than white pupils – and ten times more likely than Indian pupils. Also, black British pupils consistently earn lower grades at GCSE than white children. And only 81% of black and Asian people who have attended university have jobs, compared to 87% of white people. Government figures from 2009 also revealed that black men were almost eight times more likely to be stopped by police compared to white men, four times more likely to be arrested, and five times more likely to be in prison.

MISSION ACCOMPLISHED?

• Can you describe how three well known "Black Britons" have contributed to British society.

TASK 1 Spot the mistakes

Here are five sentences. Each sentence has two errors. One is a spelling mistake; the other is a factual error. When you have spotted each mistake, write the sentence out correctly.

a The first people to ever arrive in Britain came around 500 years ago. They were hunter-gatherers who lived by gathering food (like nuts, berrys and fruit) and killing any animals they needed.

b Around 5000 years ago the people who lived in Britain began to farm. New settlers from Europe brought seeds of wheat and barley. They also introduced animals used for meat, including pigs, sheap, goats and elephants.

c In about 2500 BC, a new wave of settlers arrived from central Europ. They were known as the Beaker People because of the decorated pottery cups they used. They knew how to make things out of copper and gold too –

and when silver was added to copper it made bronze. So the time of the Beaker People is often known as the Bronze Age.

d Over the next few thousand years, more groups arrived in Britain. Some came peacefully, to trade for example, whilst others were hostile invaders. Some came on holiday to try our beautiful beaches. Some groups came for a short while and then left, whilst others settled for good. All of them left their mark on Briton in some way.

e The five main groups that left there mark on Britain in the years up to and including 1066 were the Celts (from central Europe), the Romans (from Japan), the Anglo-Saxons (from Denmark and northern Germany), the Vikings (from Denmark, Norway and Sweden) and the Normans (from France), who conquered Britain in 1066.

TASK 2 What does it mean?

For many years, the topic of immigration has caused controversy. Some have pointed to the benefits of immigration, whilst others have argued that immigrants have contributed very little to Britain. In 2004, immigration was a particularly 'hot topic' in politics, and all the major

TV news programmes and newspapers contained stories about it. The cartoon below appeared in the Guardian newspaper in response to a story about someone who had said that Britain should be uncorrupted by the 'vile stain of immigration'?

As a class or in small groups, discuss what point you think the cartoonist was trying to make.

Try to think about the following:

- The newspaper – what does it say?

- The rat – why do you think he has been drawn in this way?

- What point is being made about immigration here?

- Do you think the cartoonist agreed that 'the vile stain of immigration' should be removed from Britain?

TASK 3 What does it mean?

This poem was written by a poet called Denniston Stewart. Read it carefully and answer the questions that follow.

It was 1948 on the Windrush ship
500 men from the Caribbean was on it
from warm Caribbean sand, to this cold English land.
We spent twenty eight day on the ship and everyone felt real sick,
couldn't take the tossing of the Windrush ship.
When we heard land ahoy, everyone packed up their one little grip [suitcase].
The ship docked at Tilbury, everyone began to feel merry setting foot in the mother country.
Looking round it wasn't jolly, not what we imagined.
The scene was drab and gloomy with plenty of chimneys that looked like factories.
And so we stepped on the hallowed British soil,
and looked forward to a future we dreamt would be better on this our English adventure.
For many the years were rough in fact it was rough and tough.
Everywhere we went what a spectacle, how we survived God knows it was a miracle,
couldn't find any place to rest our head a little.
No dogs, No Irish, No Blacks, here in the mother country Britain.
Some started working all the hours God given just to make a shilling.
Many threw pardner*
but life got harder and harder
started suffering racism in every corner.
Some got charged for murder defending themselves
against the attacker whose weapons were bicycle chains,
winkle picker, knuckle dusters.
We still held on and from the pardner we started
to get our life in some order.
We paid a deposit to the banker for our own little spot and that was that.
Things took a while to get better,
through many heart aches we had to suffer while they kept their stiff upper.
This was just a chapter because after fifty years we
remember the good and the bad, the happy and the sad
of life in the mother country.
Equality we never had, the opportunities we didn't get,
so now in our children we have our hopes and our dreams.
We the pioneers have laid a solid foundation in Britain
through blood, sweat and tears, in the heat and the cold.
There's NO Street Filled with Gold, that was just a story we were told.
The Gold is the jewel inside developed through the suffering fires of time.
So fifty years ago or fifty more to come we remember
the Empire Windrush when she first came.

*Pardner – a West Indian savings scheme

Background

a Why did West Indians come to Britain in the years after World War Two?

b What was 'Windrush'?

The poem

c According to the poet, in what ways was Britain different to what the passengers were expecting?

d Make a list of difficulties the immigrants faced when they got to Britain.

e What do you think the poet means by the lines 'so now in our children we have our hopes and our dreams. We the pioneers have laid a solid foundation'?

Extra

Can you create a series of 'freeze frames', depicting five lines or passages from the poem? In other words, create five still images or scenes based on events and/or stories from the poem.

Get your classmates to guess which lines you are depicting.

What is Britishness?

—————————— **MISSION OBJECTIVES** ——————————

- To understand what Britishness means to people
- To understand why Britishness means different things to different people
- To understand why Britishness became a political issue.

In 2005 the British government introduced new rules for people who wanted to settle in Britain and become British citizens. One rule was that they had to have a basic English language qualification. Another was that they had to pass a test about Britain, known as the 'Life in the UK Test' – a 45-minute multiple-choice exam on British society, culture and history. It covers things like Britain's laws, the history of immigration, family life in the UK, the role of local councils and services… and even where **dialects** like Geordie, Scouse and Cockney come from! To many it is known as the 'Britishness Test'. So what on earth is 'Britishness' anyway?

Britishness defined

To put it simply, Britishness is about being British. It's what binds British citizens together and makes them different from people who live in other countries. It includes the traditions, habits, symbols and types of behaviour that are familiar and common throughout Britain. These things give people who live in Britain a sense of national identity… or 'Britishness'.

SOURCE A: *These immigrants to the UK have completed all their requirements and tests and are going through the final process of becoming British citizens in London in November 2009. In 2009 over 160,000 people applied to become British citizens, of whom around 130,000 were accepted.* ⤸

Britishness as a controversial topic

The idea of Britishness has been a hot topic for many years now. Lots of people think that it is important to promote Britishness because to them 'being British' stands for good, positive values such as fairness, freedom and democracy (see Sources B and C). There have been efforts to teach more about Britishness in schools too. In a report for the *Daily Telegraph* in 2008, 51% of people surveyed thought Britishness should be a lesson in schools, and 56% felt that teaching Britishness would give children a stronger sense of national identity.

However, some people think there isn't really any such thing as Britishness. They argue that if they were born in Scotland or Wales, for example, they are Scottish or Welsh first and foremost – and British second (see Source D). Others have said that any definition of Britishness would be mainly a white, English version because this is the largest ethnic group in Britain. Some people have claimed that Britishness is in decline due to immigration, whilst others have pointed out how difficult it is to actually define it (see Source E). And it has been argued that Britishness for a white old aged pensioner in Cumbria would be very different from what being British means for a black teenager in an inner city!

WISE-UP Words

dialects

'Britain has something to say to the rest of the world about the values of freedom, democracy and the dignity of the people that you stand up for... it is important that we also remember the values we share in common.'

t **SOURCE B:** *Politician Gordon Brown, who later became the British Prime Minister, speaking in 2006.*

'We live in a very multicultural society, perhaps the most multicultural society in Europe. What actually binds us together? Well, interestingly, the thing that binds us together is Britishness.'

t **SOURCE C:** *Singer Billy Bragg, speaking in 2006.*

'I'm not sure whether there are characteristics you can define as British... be proud of your country, but define Britishness for yourself.'

t **SOURCE D:** *Minister of State for Schools and Learners, Jim Knight, speaking in 2007.*

'Britishness, meanwhile, remains a baggy concept with room for a rich assortment of cultural sympathies and identities. A man or woman can cheer for England at the World Cup, Britain at the Olympics, Europe at the Ryder Cup, Scotland against Wales, Sussex in the County Championships and the West Indies in Test matches.'

t **SOURCE E:** *From* Bloody Foreigners *by Robert Winder, Abacus, 2005.*

1. Fish and chips	11. Buckingham Palace
2. The Queen	12. Shakespeare
3. Old-fashioned pubs	13. Black cabs
4. Sunday roast	14. NHS
5. Red phone boxes	15. James Bond
6. Big Ben	16. Red Routemaster buses
7. Cream teas	17. Cheddar cheese
8. The Beatles	18. Houses of Parliament
9. The pound	19. Manchester United
10. The Royal Family	20. Ant and Dec

t **SOURCE F:** *In 2008, the* Daily Express *published their own research on the things Brits love about Britain. Their top 20 are shown here.*

However, despite all the disagreement over Britishness, several important studies have been done on what Britishness means. One of the best known studies was completed by the Commission for Racial Equality in 2005. Some of their findings are featured below.

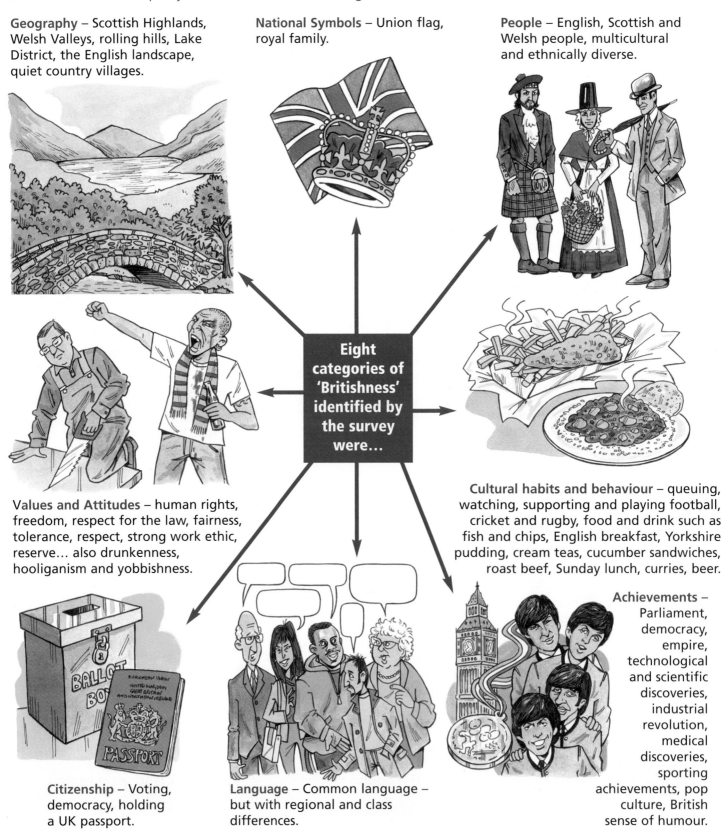

Geography – Scottish Highlands, Welsh Valleys, rolling hills, Lake District, the English landscape, quiet country villages.

National Symbols – Union flag, royal family.

People – English, Scottish and Welsh people, multicultural and ethnically diverse.

Eight categories of 'Britishness' identified by the survey were…

Values and Attitudes – human rights, freedom, respect for the law, fairness, tolerance, respect, strong work ethic, reserve… also drunkenness, hooliganism and yobbishness.

Cultural habits and behaviour – queuing, watching, supporting and playing football, cricket and rugby, food and drink such as fish and chips, English breakfast, Yorkshire pudding, cream teas, cucumber sandwiches, roast beef, Sunday lunch, curries, beer.

Citizenship – Voting, democracy, holding a UK passport.

Language – Common language – but with regional and class differences.

Achievements – Parliament, democracy, empire, technological and scientific discoveries, industrial revolution, medical discoveries, sporting achievements, pop culture, British sense of humour.

↳ **SOURCE G:** *Some of the findings of a research study carried out by the Commission for Racial Equality in 2005, called* Citizenship and Belonging: What is Britishness?

Changing ideas of being British

The topic of Britishness became even more significant after the July 2005 terror attacks on the London tube trains and a bus, in which 52 people were killed. Many people were shocked to find that the four bombers (all linked to terror group Al-Qaeda) were British citizens. One was born in Jamaica and had moved here aged five, and the other three were all born and bred in Britain, the children of Pakistani immigrants. And they had chosen to bomb symbols of British life that were typically British – the London Underground system and a red double-decker bus (see Sources H and I).

All over Britain people began asking difficult questions. What is it about British society that inspires hundreds of thousands of people to want to come and settle here – but at the same time **alienates** young British Muslims to the point where they are prepared to use terrorist bombs?

⤷ **SOURCE H:** *The fourth suicide bomb was exploded on this packed bus in Tavistock Square in London on 7 July 2005. Fourteen people, including the bomber, were killed.*

'We have to face uncomfortable facts that while the British response to July 7 was remarkable, they were British citizens, British born… who were prepared to maim and kill fellow British citizens irrespective of their religion. We have to be clearer now about how diverse cultures which contain differences can find the essential common purpose in which to flourish.'

⤷ **SOURCE I:** *Gordon Brown (the Chancellor at the time, but later Prime Minister) speaking in January 2006.*

Work

1 a What is meant by the term 'Britishness'?
   b Do you think 'Britishness' should be taught in schools? Give reasons for your answer.

2 Look at Source E.

   What point is the author, Robert Winder, trying to make here?

3 Look at Source F.
   a What is this list about?
   b In your opinion, are there any 'surprises' on the list? Are there things you wouldn't expect to be on there? Explain your choices.
   c Do you think there is anything that should be on the list that didn't get voted onto it? Explain why you think it should be in the top 20.

4 Work with a partner or in a small group. Discuss or 'brainstorm' what Britishness means to you. Design a poster, leaflet or image to show your thoughts, ideas and/or definitions.

5 a What is the 'Life in the UK Test'?
   b Devise your own 'Life in the UK Test'. What 12 questions would you ask?

—MISSION ACCOMPLISHED?—

• Can you explain what Britishness means to you?

How has immigration been portrayed on TV?

──────── MISSION OBJECTIVES ────────
• To look for ways in which the depiction of immigration and race has changed since the 1950s and 1960s.

The subjects of immigration and race have been a constant feature of television over the years. They are tackled by talk-show debates, comedy shows, soap opera storylines, documentaries and drama programmes. How immigration was covered in the early years of television? What do older shows tell us about attitudes at the time? And how has the TV portrayal of immigration changed?

Television first became popular in British homes in the 1950s. At the same time, many immigrants from former British colonies were arriving in Britain to find work. As you might expect, storylines involving immigrants soon began to appear on TV.

Making headlines

One of the first really popular TV shows to feature immigration was the ITV hospital drama *Emergency Ward 10*. This was the *Casualty* of its day and ran for 10 years from 1957. One storyline in 1964 involved a black female doctor (played by Jamaican immigrant Jan Hooley), who came to Britain to fill a vacant post. But it was the fact that she had a love affair in the show with a white doctor that made headlines – and viewers saw the first interracial kiss on British TV screens. Another love scene between the pair was banned, and later the storyline saw the doctor sent back to Africa where she was bitten by a snake and died!

↳ SOURCE B: *Til Death Us Do Part ran from 1965 to 1975, and featured a character called Alf Garnet. He was a working-class Brit who admired Enoch Powell and often voiced his prejudiced opinions about Jews, homosexuals and black immigrants. This scene shows Alf with a white actor who has 'blacked up' his face to play an Indian person! Some people at the time found Alf's views disturbing while others found it all very funny. In fact, the show's writer was trying to show how ridiculous Alf Garnet and people like him were.*

↳ SOURCE A: *Love Thy Neighbour ran from 1972 to 1976 and featured two sets of neighbours, one white and one black. It mirrored to a degree what was happening at the time as recent immigrants moved into British cities. Unusually it showed both main characters being racist to each other, and was meant to show the humour in racial tension. However, many people felt it went too far! Today it is rarely repeated, and if it is the show begins with a warning about the racist content.*

Other TV shows featuring immigrants or their descendants followed, mainly comedy shows such as *Til Death Us Do Part* and *Love Thy Neighbour*. These were mainly about racial tension between white Brits and their ethnic minority neighbours – and viewed today they seem very outdated and politically incorrect (see Sources A and B). Even *Fawlty Towers* – one of Britain's best-loved comedy shows – had a Spanish immigrant character, Manuel the waiter, who was portrayed as very stupid and got hit a lot!

Entering the mainstream

In 1978 *Empire Road* became the first British TV series to be written, acted and directed by black and Asian people. At the time it was seen as an 'ethnic' version of Coronation Street, with its portrayal of the everyday lives of African-Caribbean and Asian residents in an ordinary street. However, it only lasted for 15 shows! At the same time, a number of immigrants or their descendants began making names for themselves in British TV. Lenny Henry (the son of Jamaican immigrants) found fame as a comedian, David Yip (of East Asian descent) starred in the hit show *The Chinese Detective*, and Trevor McDonald (born in Trinidad) and Moira Stuart (of African-Caribbean descent) became key newsreaders. Another comedy show called *Desmond's* (written by a West Indian immigrant and starring a mainly black cast) became one of Channel Four's most popular British sitcom from 1989 to 1994.

In the 1980s and 1990s more shows began to reflect multicultural Britain, and actors of all races were seen in key roles on TV. Soap operas like *Coronation Street* and *EastEnders* began to include characters who were immigrants. Soaps have been criticised, however, for how some of these characters were portrayed. It has been argued, for example, that Asian characters in soaps tend to be taxi drivers or run corner shops or curry houses, while Eastern Europeans are stereotyped as builders or plumbers!

Success at last

In recent years, BBC shows like *The Kumars at No. 42* (2001–2006) and *Goodness Gracious Me* (1998–2001) have been major successes. These shows, written by British Asians, explored the conflict and comedy when traditional Asian culture clashes with modern British life. One of the famous sketches on *Goodness Gracious Me* involved a group of Indian people 'going out for an English', where they mispronounce the waiter's name, order the blandest food and ask for 24 bread rolls. It's a **parody** of a commonplace night out for British people who 'go out for an Indian', usually after heavy drinking, and order curries that are too hot and too many poppadoms! The sketch was voted in the top 10 best all-time comedy sketches in a 2008 BBC survey.

Reality TV at its best... or worst?

An interesting example of how British attitudes to immigration and race have changed since the early days of TV came in 2007. On the reality show *Celebrity Big Brother*, several housemates made nasty comments about another housemate, Indian actress Shilpa Shetty. As a result Channel Four received 55,000 complaints from viewers, and the media picked up the story and labelled it a 'race row'. The ringleader of the racism – Jade Goody – struggled to find work again after the show, her media career in ruins.

WISE-UP Words

parody

Work

1 Write out the years listed below in the correct chronological order. Next to each year write down what memorable or significant TV event relating to race and immigration happened that year.
1965   1998   1957   1972   1964
2007   2978   1989   2001

2 Look at Sources A and B
  a Does the popularity of these shows prove that all British people at this time had racist attitudes? Explain your answer carefully.
  b Why do you think these two shows are rarely repeated on television today?

3 a When talking about race, what does the word 'stereotypical' mean?
  b Make a list of as many black and Asian characters as you can think of in popular soap operas like *Coronation Street* and *EastEnders*. Write down the jobs they do and/or their family situations. Do your findings support the view that soap operas tend to portray characters in a stereotypical way?

4 What does the Big Brother 'race row' of 2007 show us about the change in attitudes towards race and immigration since the 1960s and 1970s?

MISSION ACCOMPLISHED?

• Can you explain how the depiction of immigration and race on TV has changed since the earliest days of TV in Britain?

SOUTH ASIAN IMMIGRATION

For years Britain's favourite meal was a Sunday roast or fish and chips, but in the 1990s things started to change. Curry, a food brought to Britain by immigrants from India, Pakistan and Bangladesh (an area often known as South Asia), began to increase in popularity. Soon chicken tikka masala had become the country's best-selling ready-meal. In fact, in a famous speech in 2001, politician Robin Cook said that 'chicken tikka masala is now the true British national dish'. The popularity of this food, brought to Britain by immigrants, is a classic example of the impact that immigration from South Asia has had on Britain. This Depth Study traces the origins of immigration from South Asia, and considers how it has contributed to British culture.

1: Lascars, curry and shampoo

_____ MISSION OBJECTIVES _____

- To recall how 'lascars' and 'ayahs' relate to the reasons why many South Asians first came to Britain in the 1700s and 1800s.

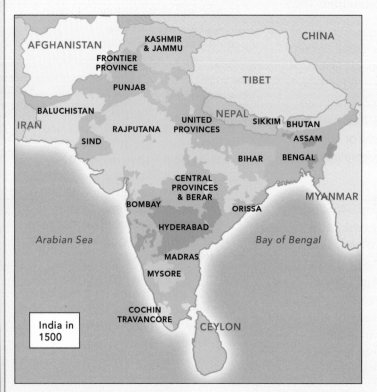

↰ SOURCE A: *South Asia in 1500 when 'India' was part of the British Empire.*

Britain and South Asia

The relationship between Britain and South Asia goes back hundreds of years. Today South Asia is a collection of separate countries including India, Pakistan, Bangladesh, Sri Lanka and Burma, but back then it was all called '**India**' by the British. In the early 1600s British traders went there to buy spices, dyes and textiles to sell back in Britain. Over the next 250 years British traders built 'trading posts' along the South Asian coast, and gradually Britain took over more and more of the land. After a huge rebellion against foreign rule in 1857, the British government decided to put 'India' under its own direct control. Queen Victoria even proudly called herself 'Empress of India'.

South Asians in Britain

South Asians have been coming to Britain since the early days of British rule in 'India'. Many worked as cooks, deckhands and sailors on board ships bringing goods to Britain. These South Asian sailors were called **lascars** (see Source B). Between voyages most lascars settled near the London docks and took on other jobs. They ran lodging houses for other sailors, set up cafes or tea shops along the waterfront, or became market traders.

But sailors weren't the only South Asian immigrants to settle in Britain. There were also **ayahs** (children's nannies) and servants of wealthy British families who had lived out in South Asia but decided to return home to Britain. In fact, by the 1800s, it was estimated that there were around 40,000 South Asians in Britain – mainly lascars, but also ayahs, servants, students, officials, doctors, tourists and businessmen.

Curry, spice and all things nice

As British control of South Asia grew, so did interest in South Asian food back in Britain. 'Curry' first appeared on an English menu in 1773 at the Norris Street Coffee Shop in Haymarket, London. A few years later, in 1809, Britain's very first Indian restaurant was opened at 34 George Street, Portman Square, London. It was called the Hindostanee Coffee House and was run by a Bengali immigrant named Sake Dean Mohamed.

WISE-UP Words

ayah

India   lascar

By the late 1800s there were around 70,000 South Asians – or descendents of South Asians – in Britain, and they were beginning to make an impact in all sorts of ways (see Sources C, D and E).

SOURCE B: *Mohamed's Baths opened in 1814. It offered a 'shampooing vapour medicated massage bath' to cure many diseases such as stiff joints, sprains, aches and pains. Before Mohamed came to Britain, Brits had never heard of the word 'shampoo'! Mohamed even became the 'shampooing surgeon' to both King George IV and King William IV.* ↱

↳ **SOURCE C:** *Kumar Shri Ranjitsinhji ('Rangji') was born in India in 1872 and moved to Britain in 1891. He captained Sussex Country Cricket Team for 19 years and in 1896 became the first Indian to represent England at cricket – and scored a century in his first Test! He scored another century in his first 'away' Test in another country too, a feat not repeated until Andrew Strauss did it in 2004, 108 years later!*

Work

1 If you were to ask Queen Victoria to describe what she understood by the word 'India', what do you think she would say?

2 Explain why you think Sake Dean Mohamed, Kumar Shri Ranjitsinhji and Sophia Duleep Singh have been chosen to appear on these pages?

3 a What is meant by the term 'national dish'?

   b Compile a list of contenders for 'Britain's National Dish', perhaps five or ten choices. You might do this with a partner or as a class. Then put the foods you have chosen in an order, with your favourite choice for 'Britain's National Dish' at the top. Explain why and how you have made your decision.

   c Try to work out where each of the choices on your list originated from.

SOURCE D: *Sophia Duleep Singh, daughter of an Indian Sikh prince and his African-German wife, was born in Suffolk in 1876. She is pictured here selling the* Suffragette *outside Hampton Court Palace. Singh was prominent in the fight for women's rights – in particular the right to vote – in the early 1900s.* ↱

MISSION ACCOMPLISHED?

• Can you explain what is meant by the terms 'lascar', 'ayah' and 'South Asian'?

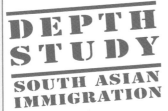

People from India, Pakistan, Bangladesh and Sri Lanka (South Asia) have been moving to Britain for hundreds of years. The largest groups were in London – and were mainly Indian sailors – but in other places such as Oxford, Bristol and Cambridge there were South Asian students, servants and nannies too. As early as 1688, a man in Bristol offered a reward of 20 shillings (about £90 now) for the safe return of his 'runaway Indian'. But it was in the 1950s and 1960s that really large numbers of South Asian immigrants began coming to Britain. By 1971 the number of immigrants from South Asia had reached around 400,000 people, equal to about 1% of the total population. So why did so many South Asians migrate to Britain? What did they do when they got here? What were attitudes like at the time to this immigration? And how have South Asian communities contributed to British life?

2: The South Asian experience

MISSION OBJECTIVES

- To understand why many South Asians chose to move to Britain in the 1950s and 1960s… and how they were treated when they got here.

Enough jobs for all?

There were a number of reasons why thousands of South Asians came to settle in Britain after World War Two ended:

- There was violence in some parts of South Asia after the war, and some immigrants came to Britain to avoid this.

- The people of many South Asian countries, including India, Pakistan and Bangladesh, were British passport holders and so had the right to come and live in Britain if they wanted to. These countries used to be part of the British Empire so everyone living there qualified for a British passport.

- Some places in South Asia suffered from cyclones, floods and famines at this time – and terrible poverty. Many people living in these areas saw emigration as their only hope.

However, the vast majority of South Asians who came to Britain in the 1950s and 1960s came for one reason only – jobs! Some of the immigrants had professional qualifications – for example, many were doctors who came to work in Britain's hospitals. But most were unskilled workers who were invited over to Britain to take a job in one of Britain's key industries, many of which were experiencing a labour shortage after the war. Soon, thousands of South Asians had taken jobs at Wolf's Rubber Factory in Southall, near London, or at Heathrow Airport. There were also lots of jobs at iron foundries in Birmingham, steelworks in Scunthorpe and Sheffield, and textile mills in northern towns such as Bolton, Bradford and Manchester (see Source A).

SOURCE A: *A South Asian immigrant at work in a textile mill in Bradford.* ⤹

! FACT African expulsion

As well as coming from South Asia itself, thousands of Indians and Pakistanis arrived in Britain in the 1960s after Kenya expelled them. In 1972 Ugandan President Idi Amin expelled around 70,000 Ugandan Asians – and Britain agreed to take 21,000 immigrants. There was public alarm at the time, with various different groups and politicians arguing that Britain couldn't cope with all the new immigrants. Leicester City Council even placed adverts in Ugandan newspapers urging the Asians to stay away!

The next generation

Many of the South Asian immigrants came to Britain alone at first, often leaving their wives and families behind them. After a few years, most would ask their families to come over to Britain to join them. Some of the single men married local British women. In time, as their children were born in Britain, a 'second generation' of South Asians emerged. A government report of 1960 recorded a total of 34,000 Indian children and 5,000 Pakistani children in Britain – and around 64% of them had been born there! This next generation regarded themselves as British Asians (see Source B).

'I'm British – end of story! I was born in Britain and I've lived all my life here. I dress like I'm British, sound like I'm British, have a mix of mates from all cultures – but I certainly see myself as a Brit first, a British Asian yes, but I'm British first and foremost!'

⤶ **SOURCE B:** *Sukhjinder Singh, a British Asian student from the West Midlands, speaking in 2010. His mother was born in Britain and his father was born in India. All his grandparents were Indian immigrants in the 1960s.*

British life

The experience of starting a new life in Britain varied enormously for South Asian immigrants. Some settled in straight away, working hard, setting up businesses and achieving a great deal. The earlier arrivals moved into areas that were previously 'all-white' and some tried to 'fit in' immediately by wearing western fashions, learning English as quickly as possible and making English friends. This sometimes led to tensions within some immigrant households, especially if there were older family members who wanted to preserve their South Asian customs, traditions and dress.

Other new immigrants found Britain tough. They struggled to adapt to the way of life, missed home and suffered racial abuse. For many new immigrants it must have seemed like a 'no-win' situation! Any immigrants without jobs were accused of being lazy and 'living off the state'. But those with jobs were accused of 'taking jobs off English people'! Sources C, D, E and F illustrate some of the varied experiences of South Asian immigrants in Britain.

'We are bothered about our lives. White children kick us and scream abuse. Bottles are thrown. We are threatened by the National Front [a racist group]. The other day my wife and I had a light bulb thrown at us while we were walking down the street.'

↳ **SOURCE E:** *Muhammed Huque, quoted in the* Daily Mail, *6 August 1978 (from* Past Into Present 3 *by Fisher and Williams, Collins, 1989).*

'In the early years, my mother dressed us like the English. My brother and I associated with English friends. As our parents did not want us to be different in any way, they made sure we learned English properly. When our relatives came, everything changed. The women would come to our house and say "Don't you think Nimi's hair should be braided now that she is ten?" or "Nimi should not go to school with bare legs, otherwise she will grow up immodest". Immediately my mother's attitude changed. I was no longer to be like the English, but was to dress like the Punjabi villagers –

↳ **SOURCE F:** *A Sikh woman remembering her life, 1979 (from* A Nation of Immigrants, *J.D. Clare, Hodder, 2010).*

'When I first arrived the local people generally didn't like us. Once I remember being confronted by a white man telling me "you lot are good for nothing. You come over here, take our jobs and we don't like you". I told him that it was my country too, I had fought for it and if we had been late getting to the battlefront this country would have been in the hands of the Germans.'

↳ **SOURCE C:** *Mohamed Zaman Khan (quoted on the website www.movinghere.org.uk) talking about his experiences upon arrival in Britain. He refers to his contribution fighting for Britain in World War Two.*

'Having a shop gave me a very close contact and friendship with everyone... they came to share their gossip, their sorrows and joys, so I learnt about English society very quickly... it was a friendly atmosphere, we knew the whole street.'

↳ **SOURCE D:**
Mrs Hussain (quoted on www.movinghere.org.uk) talking about how well she was received by her new white neighbours in Wandsworth, London, upon arrival in the UK in the early 1960s.

Restaurants and corner shops

In the 1970s and 1980s many of Britain's factories, mills and steelworks closed down. As a result, thousands of people in Britain lost their jobs – including a lot of South Asian immigrants and their descendants. However, many South Asians were determined to keep working hard, and a lot of them decided to set up their own small businesses. In 1974 only 8% of South Asians were self-employed, but by 1991 that figure had risen to 26%. In 1960 there were around 500 'curry-houses' in Britain – but by 1980 there were 3,000, and by 2010 there were around 9,000 South Asian restaurants and take-aways. Over £2 billion a year is spent in them and they employ around 70,000 people!

However, the majority of small businesses started by South Asians in the last 30 years have been small shops – or 'corner shops' as they are **stereotypically** known. In 1992 it was estimated that around 70% of sweet shops, grocers and newsagents in Britain were owned by South Asians. In order to compete with the large supermarkets, the shopkeepers had to 'open all hours' – yet they continue to thrive. They provide a local and convenient service, which is especially important for the elderly and for non-drivers.

↰ **SOURCE G:** *In 1992 it was estimated that 70% of 'corner shops' and newsagents were owned by South Asians.*

Work

1 Make a list of reasons why many South Asians came to settle in Britain after World War Two ended.

2 Look at Source C.
  a Why was Mohamed Khan confronted by the 'white man'?
  b How did Mohamed Khan respond?
  c What is your opinion about Mohamed Khan's response? Do you think it had any effect on the white man?

3 Look at Sources D and E.
  a In what ways do the two sources differ?
  b Can you think of reasons why the experiences of these two South Asian families were so different?

4 Look at Source F.
  a Why was the Sikh woman so upset about the arrival of her relatives?
  b Why do you think many South Asian immigrants tried to keep some of their 'home' traditions and cultural habits when they came to live in Britain?

5 In what ways, in particular, have South Asian immigrants contributed to small business enterprise in the last 30 years?

— **MISSION ACCOMPLISHED?** —

• How successful do you think South Asian immigration to the UK was in the twentieth century?

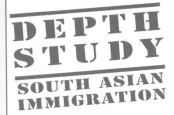

Many of the South Asian immigrants who arrived in the 1950s and 1960s made Britain their home. Their children, grandchildren (and even great-grandchildren) were born in Britain and now regard themselves as British – or British Asians. Today there are around 4 million people of South Asian origin in Britain – around 1.6 million of Indian descent, 1 million of Pakistani and Bangladeshi descent and around 100,000 Sri Lankans. Descendants of other South Asian areas such as Nepal or the Maldives have settled in Britain too. The main religions of British Asians are Islam, Hinduism and Sikhism.

3: Modern British Asians

MISSION OBJECTIVES

• To assess how significant South Asian immigration has been to British culture and society.

The impact of South Asian immigration on life in Britain has been immense, and in all sorts of areas. For example, in healthcare the contribution of South Asians has been very important – today around 20% of hospital doctors, 16% of GPs and 12% of pharmacists are of South Asian descent. Indeed, many of the first South Asian doctors who arrived in Britain in the 1950s and 1960s took jobs in poorer areas of large cities and towns where there was a shortage of doctors (see Source A).

'Britain could not live as she does without her immigrants. The health service would break down; roughly 40 per cent of the doctors in British hospitals up to consultant level come from overseas; the greater part from India and Pakistan.'

↳ SOURCE A: *From* The Times *newspaper, 1966.*

ENTERPRISE

Their willingness to work long, unsociable hours has seen South Asian shopkeepers revitalize struggling corner shops. Many are profitable businesses that are 'open all hours' for the convenience of their local communities. Further, South Asian businessmen and women have been very successful in all kinds of industries; for example, steel manufacturing, clothing and fashion, property and IT.

Entrepreneur and multimillionaire James Caan (born Nazim Khan in Pakistan in 1960) moved to Britain with his family in 1962. He has become one of Britain's most successful businessmen, owning a number of recruitment firms and appearing in the BBC series *Dragons' Den*. In July 2010 it was revealed that, at the time, another South Asian – Lakshmi Mittal (born in India but now living in London) – was Britain and Europe's richest man, and one of the world's top ten richest. He made his fortune in steel-making.

The South Asian influence is evident in food (curry is one of Britain's favourite take-away and home-cooked meals) and fashion, from nose-rings to pashminas. Indeed, it has been estimated that British Asians, who make up around 4% of the population, contribute 6% to Britain's GDP (Gross Domestic Product, this is the amount of money the country makes). Sources B, C and D further explore the South Asian contribution to British life.

❗ **FACT** Education

The educational achievements of children of South Asian descent are mixed. Students of Indian or mixed Indian origin consistently perform better than all other groups (including White British) at GCSE and A level, and are more likely to have University degrees. Those of Pakistani and Bangladeshi descent generally perform worse than both white British and Indian students – but better than Black Caribbean or Black African students. However, in recent years GCSE results have been rising for all British Asians.

SPORT

SOURCE B: *British sport has benefitted from South Asian immigration for many years. England's cricket team has been captained by Nasser Hussain (who was born in India to an Indian father and an English mother) and pictured here is bowler Monty Panesar (fourth from right, born in Britain to immigrants from India in the 1970s), and all-rounder Dimitri Mascarenhas (second from right, of Sri Lankan heritage). Other notable British Asian sportsmen include boxer Amir Khan (Olympic Silver medallist and World Champion) and footballer Zesh Rehman (the first British Asian to play in all four top divisions of English football).* ↱

! FACT Racial tension

Racial tension still exists in some British communities, and between all ethnic groups, not just white and non-white. For example, violence against British Asian Muslims increased after the London Bombings of 2005 when a terror attack against London Transport was carried out by three British Asians of Pakistani descent and one Jamaican-born man. There have been isolated examples of extreme violence in places in the UK such as "race riots" in Bradford in 2001, and in 2005 there was fighting between the Black British and South Asian British communities in Birmingham.

MUSIC

↰ **SOURCE C:** *One of the first British Asian musicians to gain worldwide fame was Freddie Mercury (born Farrokh Bulsara to Indian immigrant parents). He was the lead singer of rock band Queen who had massive hits in the 1970s and 1980s with songs such as Bohemian Rhapsody, Don't Stop Me Now and We Will Rock You. In 2005 an MTV survey voted him the greatest male singer of all time. In 2009 Jay Sean (born Kamaljit Singh Jhooti in London to Punjabi Sikh immigrants) became the first British Asian solo artist to reach number 1 in the US pop charts.*

TV AND FILM

↰ **SOURCE D:** *In arts and the media many British Asians have made their mark. Writers such as Salman Rushdie, Meera Syal and Hanif Kureshi have topped the best seller lists and won literary awards. British Asian comedy shows and dramas (such as Goodness Gracious Me and The Kumars at No. 42) have won prime time TV slots and numerous TV awards. More journalists, reporters and news presenters of South Asian origin are gaining prominence too. In recent years films such as East is East, Bend it Like Beckham and Oscar-winning Slumdog Millionaire (pictured here) have made it to the mainstream.*

Work ⌇

1 In your own words, explain what is meant by the term 'British Asians'.

2 a Describe how South Asian immigrants and their descendants have affected British:
   i healthcare
   ii food and diet
   iii sport
   iv music
   v business and the economy.
   b For each category, explain if you think that the effect has been positive (a good thing) or negative (a bad thing).

3 Many immigrants of South Asian origin have become quite wealthy and successful through hard work and good management. Yet some non-Asian people resent their success. Try to explain why.

— MISSION ACCOMPLISHED? —

• Can you make a list of the ways in which South Asians have contributed to the British way of life?

How has immigration changed Britain?

___MISSION OBJECTIVES___

- To answer the question: 'What have the immigrants ever done for Britain?'

Different groups of people of different nationalities have been moving to Britain for many years. Britain is now the home of people from lots of different ethnic backgrounds and cultures. In fact, many people now call Britain a 'multicultural' society.

The impact of immigration upon Britain and the British way of life has been dramatic – influencing everything from the music we listen to, to the way we speak and the food we eat. Our high streets, housing estates, hospitals, schools and sports teams have all been affected by the diversity of the different cultures that live in Britain. In fact, it is hard to imagine what life in Britain would be like without the influence of immigration.

A There are around 9,000 Indian restaurants and 14,000 Chinese takeaways in Britain today.

B In Britain today, around one-fifth of students in schools are from ethnic minorities.

C Around one in eight of the British workforce was born abroad.

D Some parts of the 'full English breakfast' have overseas origins – like sausages (Germany), baked beans (America) and black pudding (brought to England by European monks).

E Fish and chips is still one of Britain's best loved foods – but the first fish and chip shop was opened in 1860 in London by a Jewish immigrant.

F Pizza, which originated as a cheap meal for poor people in Italy, has been adopted as one of Britain's best-selling fast foods. Kebabs, another popular choice, are Turkish.

G Tea, one of Britain's favourite drinks, originated in China and was first brought to Britain in the 1600s. Coffee arrived in the same century.

K Mosques, temples and synagogues are now a common sight in towns and cities.

L Some say the NHS could not survive without the contribution of immigration. Around 20% of hospital doctors and 16% of GPs are of South Asian descent. And around 30% of all the doctors in the UK today are foreign-born.

Immigration has made its mark on the English language. Everyday words from other places include: chocolate, potato and tomato (South Asian); barbecue (Caribbean); zombie (West African); chemistry, cotton and assassin (Arabic); bangle and shampoo (Hindi); pal (Romany) and tycoon (Japanese). Over 200 languages are spoken in Britain today.

Work

1 Write a sentence or two to explain what you think is meant by the term 'multicultural Britain'?

2 Look at the picture and labels on this page.
   a What do the picture and labels show?
   b Make a list of all the ways in which the different immigrant and ethnic influences shown in the diagram directly affect you personally today. For example, do you drink tea… or is pizza your favourite food… or fish and chips… or is the doctor you see of South Asian descent?
   c Can you think of any other ways that your life – or life of Britain in general – is affected by ethnic or immigrant influences?

H Around 12% of pharmacists in Britain are of Indian, Pakistani or Bangladeshi descent.

I Tesco, Britain's largest supermarket chain, was started by the son of a Polish Jewish immigrant.

J In the 1800s, hundreds of thousands of Irish immigrants helped to build Britain's new networks of roads, railways and canals. In 2001, a survey found that 42% of English people had some Irish blood.

MISSION ACCOMPLISHED?

• Can you list eight ways in which immigration has changed Britain?

Why is immigration such a controversial subject?

MISSION OBJECTIVES

• To analyse the arguments surrounding the topic of immigration and develop your own opinion on the subject.

There is no doubt that the topic of immigration is very controversial. In schools, homes and workplaces all over Britain the issue of immigration is regularly discussed, argued over and even shouted about. Immigration-related stories and reports often appear in newspapers and feature heavily in TV news programmes and documentaries. During the 2010 UK General Election, immigration was identified by voters in surveys as one of the top three issues affecting Britain. So why does this topic arouse such strong emotions and fierce debate?

The key issue

The reason why immigration is such a controversial subject is straightforward – it is a very, very **divisive** issue. In other words, to some people immigration is a real problem that needs to be dealt with, whilst for others it isn't a problem at all! A 2010 survey for a UK national newspaper highlighted this. It showed that nearly 70% of people interviewed felt that immigration had a negative impact on Britain and that there were too many immigrants coming in… but around 30% felt that immigration had a positive effect on the country and that the number of immigrants being allowed in was fine!

The key arguments

People who are against immigration, or believe it should be more tightly controlled, generally make several key points. These include:

• Immigrants take jobs from British workers – and if they haven't got a job, they claim benefits!

• Britain cannot afford to take in all the immigrants from other countries that want to be here. Britain is already crowded – and its housing, education and health services cannot take the strain of even more people.

• Immigration is making Britain lose its national identity. Parts of the country don't even feel like Britain anymore, mainly because immigrants isolate themselves in their own communities and refuse to learn the language!

However, typical responses to these arguments include:

• Immigrants do not 'steal jobs' from British workers. They often take the tough, dirty, low-paid jobs that most British workers won't do – or make up shortages in highly skilled professions such as medicine.

• Most immigrants are of working age so they pay tax and spend money on goods and services like everyone else. As taxpayers, they're entitled to use Britain's health service and education system, just like Brits are… and those without jobs should be able to go to a doctor for free on the NHS, just like an unemployed British person can!

• Britain's national identity is always changing. The idea that immigrants are 'ruining' it is nonsense. Britain's identity has been built up over the centuries and lots of cultures have contributed to it. Immigrants have brought a huge amount of culture, wealth and ideas to Britain.

As you can see, immigration is such a controversial topic because opinions on it are so divided. Sources A to H illustrate this.

'Immigration has damaged community relations in parts of England, a report by the government says. In three areas with high immigration – Peterborough, Burnley, and Barking and Dagenham – **community cohesion** [togetherness] is among the lowest in the country, the MPs say. The report said there was "significant public anxiety" over issues such as pressure on public services.'

⤶ SOURCE A: *From a BBC online article entitled 'Immigration Harming Communities', 16 July 2008.*

'Most immigrants are of working age, which means they consume less of the services provided by the State, such as healthcare and education, and pay more in taxes. In the UK, Home Office research suggests that immigrants pay £2.5 billion more in taxes than they take in benefits. And they estimate that economic growth has been boosted because of immigration.'

⤶ SOURCE B: *From a BBC website, 14 January 2008.*

Sam (an unemployed 19-year-old who has been looking for work): 'I even went to see if I could do cabbage picking but because all the foreigners [immigrant workers] were on it, they said, we've got them cheaper than you.'

⤴ **SOURCE C:** *From a TV documentary called 'The Day the Immigrants Left', screened in February 2010.*

'What about rich countries, like America and Britain, now bursting with foreigners? The benefits should be obvious: our economies are bigger, stronger and more flexible with immigrants than without them. Immigrants expand the workforce, and drive up economic growth, meaning more taxes to pay for public services, more demand in the economy in general; immigrants release the natives [British people] from the drudge work like fruit picking, caring for the elderly, nannying, to do something more rewarding; highly-skilled immigrants do jobs for which there are too few skilled natives (plumbers, electricians, doctors, traders, bankers).'

⤴ **SOURCE D:** *From an article by Adam Roberts in the Guardian newspaper online, 4 January 2008, entitled 'More Migrants Please'. Interestingly, since 2004 the number of immigrants from Eastern European countries had increased dramatically – but then, in 2009, more Eastern Europeans left Britain than arrived!*

'A migration think tank claims UK schools spend nearly £13 million a day to educate the children of migrants. The figure was quoted in a report by Migrationwatch, published in October 2010... in its latest report on the impact of immigration on schools, Migrationwatch stated over half a million more school places will be needed by 2015 for the children of recent immigrants to the UK.'

⤴ **SOURCE E:** *From a BBC Cambridgeshire online article called 'Immigration: The cost for schools', 15 October 2010. The 'think tank' quoted in the article (Migrationwatch) is opposed to the levels of immigration seen in Britain in recent years.*

⭐ WISE-UP Words

community cohesion   divisive

Interviewer: 'The key question is – does the education of local children suffer as a result of immigration?'
Headteacher: 'It's unequivocal [very clear] – no! No! Nobody suffers, everybody gains.'
Interviewer: 'How was the school rated by OFSTED before the new arrivals – and how is it rated now? Has there been a deterioration? Or improvement?'
Headteacher: 'We've been "good, with aspects of outstanding", for the last two OFSTEDS; we were "good" before that.'

⤴ **SOURCE F:** *Interview with primary school headteacher, Lesley Mardle, as part of the TV programme 'The Day the Immigrants Left'. Overall the programme showed that immigration brought many benefits to the area it focused on (Wisbech in Cambridgeshire), but also pointed out some of the strains the influx of immigrants put on local services like schools and doctors.*

'Put it this way, if all the immigrants went home tomorrow, this area would collapse. There would be no one to do the work! It's alright people saying they're taking all the jobs, but there's no British workers to do them... and I pay the foreign workers the same rate – they don't do it any cheaper.'

⤴ **SOURCE G:** *Colin, a property owner and builder from Wisbech, featured in a BBC documentary.*

'You used to be able to go and see a doctor the same day, now you have to wait 10 days to get an appointment and all the schools are packed out with children... I just think they're taking and they've nothing to give.'

⤴ **SOURCE H:** *From interviews in the documentary 'The Day the Immigrants Left'.*

Work

1 Choose 4 sources from these pages. For each one say whether the source supports (is in favour of) immigration, or whether it is against (is quite negative about) immigration. For each source, explain in your own words the point that the source is trying to make.

2 Work with a partner to create a conversation between two people – one in favour of and one against immigration. What are the main points of the conversation? What do you disagree over the most? Do you agree about anything?

The key facts and figures

Britain has a long history of immigration (people coming into the country) and emigration (people leaving). Up until the 1980s there were more people moving out of Britain (to places like Australia, Canada, Spain and New Zealand) than coming into the country. Since then, things have changed (see Source I).

As Source I shows, since the early 1990s more and more people have been coming to live in Britain. In 2009, for example, 567,000 people settled in Britain – and 371,000 left. This left a *net* figure of 196,000 people... so Britain's population *increased* by several hundred thousand due to migration in 2009! Interestingly, the number of people coming into Britain in 2009 actually decreased compared to the previous year (down 4%)... but fewer people left, so the net figure still *increased* by 33,000 compared to 2008.

Using statistics

As you might imagine, people (especially journalists and politicians) seize on these yearly immigration figures and can skilfully twist the numbers to back up whatever point they want to make. For example, if a politician wanted to use the figures in Source I to argue that immigration is 'out of control', they might say that 'the graph shows a rapid rise in immigration over the last 20 years, which is a result of us letting more people into Britain'. However, someone wishing to argue that immigration is 'under control' might say that 'since 2004 immigration to Britain has been steady. In fact, immigration dropped in 2009, which shows that the government has it under control'.

In 2009 the people coming into Britain included:

- 193,000 people coming to work here with work permits (the vast majority from European Union countries or former Commonwealth countries like India, Pakistan and Nigeria).

- Around 100,000 arriving to either join or accompany their family.

- 211,000 people who were granted permission to study here.

- Around 20,000 applicants for asylum (generally around 70% are refused asylum each year and many remain in the country illegally).

It is estimated now that around 6 million people living in Britain were born abroad. In 1981 this figure was around 2 million. But Britain is not the only country that has seen an increase in immigration – and the issue is just as controversial in other countries too. Australia, for example,

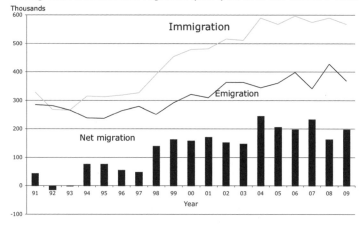

Long-Term International Migration (LTIM) to/from the UK 1991-2009

SOURCE I: *A graph showing net migration into Britain, 1991–2009. Net migration is the final change in population after all the people leaving Britain (emigrating) and all the people moving into Britain (immigrating) have been taken into account. As you can see from the graph, since around 1993, far more people have come into Britain than have left, so net migration has increased.*

SOURCES J AND K: *It is estimated that around 6 million people living in Britain were born abroad.*

has the largest share of immigrants in its population with 24%, followed by Germany (13%), the USA (12.8%) and France (10%). Recent British government statistics have estimated that the population of Britain will reach 65 million in 2023 and 70 million by 2031 if the current rate of immigration continues! Many politicians and commentators have spoken out against the numbers of people allowed to move to Britain – and have called for a very strict limit to be set for the numbers allowed in.

The impact

In 2007, the government set up a group called the Migration Impacts Forum (MIF). It was made up of people from local councils who would meet regularly to report on the impact of immigration in their area. Their first report, in October 2007, said:

- Immigration benefits Britain overall.

- Immigrants made an important contribution in many areas of work, especially farm work, care work and in hospitals.

- Five regions out of eight reported an increase in the number of pupils at their schools who did not speak English as a first language.

- Four areas out of eight reported an increase in demand for housing.

- Two regions reported increased pressure on doctors.

- Five regions reported an increase in low-level crime (such as not wearing a seatbelt, for example).

- Two regions reported some increase in community tension.

- Six regions said they were concerned that immigrants would be cheated by their employers or landlords.

Immigration is a controversial topic. Can you see how these two photographs portray immigrants in different ways?

With a topic as controversial as immigration, it's no surprise that this report was viewed (or interpreted) in different ways by different people. Some thought it proved that immigration to the UK was a positive thing for the country… whilst others argued that it showed immigration was placing a huge strain on Britain! Can you see why this report was interpreted in different ways?

WISE-UP Words

illegal immigration

net migration

! FACT How many?

One of the most controversial aspects of the immigration debate is **illegal immigration**. Illegal immigrants are people who come to Britain by illegal means (smuggled into the country hidden in lorries, for example). They have no proper documentation and have not applied to be here through the proper channels. In 2009, one estimate suggested that there may be as many as one million 'illegals' living in Britain! In some areas, it is the illegal immigrant issue that sparks the fiercest debate.

Work

1 Look at Source I
  a What does this source show?
  b What is meant by the term 'interpretation'?
  c In what ways could this source be interpreted in different ways?

2 In 2009, for what purpose and for what reasons did different groups of people come to Britain? Give figures to support your answer.

3 Look at Sources J and K.
  a In what ways are the two photographs different in the way they portray immigration?
  b Which photograph would you use if you were writing an article about the benefits and the positive side of immigration? Explain how you made your choice.

MISSION ACCOMPLISHED?

- If someone asked you why the topic of immigration is so controversial, would you be able to explain?

Should immigration be stopped?

_____ MISSION OBJECTIVES _____

- To identify what you think are the *three* main arguments in favour of immigration and the *three* main arguments against it.

Over the years there have been many different rules, regulations and laws on immigration in Britain. It remains one of the most controversial and hotly debated issues in British politics, classrooms, newspapers and homes. One question that is asked more and more often these days is this one – should immigration be stopped altogether?

In 2009, Britain's population increased at its fastest rate in 50 years. It's because high immigration levels have meant more women of childbearing age. Immigrant families are bigger on average too. Our schools can't take the amount of children! And it's stretching healthcare services and causing housing shortages.

Immigrants *do* "take our jobs", but most of those jobs are in the "3D" category – dirty, dangerous or difficult. If immigrants didn't do them, who would?

Our communities are being destroyed by immigration. In 2008, a survey showed that 58% of Brits felt that parts of this country don't feel like Britain anymore because of immigration. It's just wrong to have to feel like a stranger in your own country.

Millions of Brits have gone to live in places like Canada, Australia and Spain. It's hypocritical to say we can move abroad but people shouldn't be allowed to move here!

I've nothing against people who come here to escape famine or persecution, but why do asylum seekers pass through other safe countries like France, Germany and Italy to get here? It's because they know we're a soft touch, that's why! We give them more benefits!

It's been shown that immigrants pay more in taxes than they take out in benefits – so we actually make money from immigration! The idea that immigrants just take from us and give nothing back is totally false.

We're a rich, privileged nation and we're rightly proud of our record on human rights, justice, democracy and freedom. How could we refuse to allow people who are persecuted or starving to come here and be safe?

We're already a crowded country – we simply can't take any more immigrants. At this rate Britain's population will be over 70 million by 2031. We'll be one of Europe's most populated countries – and we're only a quarter of the size of France.

Britain has a tradition of adopting ideas from other cultures. Our national religion began in the Middle East and was brought here by monks, and our language is a mixture from various other places. Even England's patron saint (St George) was a Roman soldier from Turkey! If you go back far enough, all Britons are immigrants really.

It's wrong to say Britain has a history of immigration going back thousands of years. The Celts, Romans, Saxons and so on weren't "immigrants" – they were invaders! And after 1066 only small groups came. It's only recently that immigrants have come in their millions.

Police in some areas have noticed a rise in crime due to the sudden increase in immigrants. In Cambridgeshire, drink-driving figures showed a 17-fold rise in arrests of foreigners in one year.

Look at what immigrants have contributed to British banking, literature, business, music, food and sport. Immigration has added so much to British culture. You can't enjoy a Chinese takeaway, drink tea, or shop in Marks & Spencer or Tesco, and then say immigration has brought us nothing and should be stopped!

Work

Either Write an essay entitled 'Should immigration be stopped'? A good essay will have a beginning, a middle and an end. In other words, it should start with an introduction on the topic which outlines key facts and figures on immigration. Then you should provide details of the key arguments for and against immigration, ensuring you outline a balanced view of the topic. You should also include a conclusion, perhaps detailing your own personal opinion on immigration in a structured and appropriate way.

Or Divide the class into two groups – one group 'for' and another 'against' stopping immigration. Work as a group or with a partner within your group to discuss ways to present your argument that support your view. You might wish to look through the book to help you with facts, figures an details.

Then, as a whole class, hold a debate called 'Should immigration be stopped'?

MISSION ACCOMPLISHED?

• Could you take part in a discussion or debate on the topic of immigration and be able to outline both sides of the argument?

TASK 1 Interpretation – melting pot, salad bowl or tomato soup?

People often use analogies when talking about the impact of immigration on British society. An analogy is a comparison between two different things in order to show how they are similar. Three analogies of the impact of immigration on Britain are the 'melting pot', the 'salad bowl' and 'tomato soup'!

British society has sometimes been described as a 'melting pot'. The idea behind the analogy is that the 'pot' (Britain) contains lots of different ingredients (people of different races and cultures) who bring all sorts of flavours (foods, traditions, beliefs, etc.) with them to combine (melt) into the final meal (British society).

The 'salad bowl' analogy is similar to the 'melting pot' in some ways. Britain is still represented as a bowl, but the different ingredients (the different races and cultures) do not melt together to form one mixture – instead, they keep their own flavours. This suggests that different cultures and identities are still easily identified in Britain, just like the different ingredients are easily identified in a salad.

The 'tomato soup' analogy is a new one. It uses the fact that tomato soup is based on one ingredient, but others are added to it (salt, pepper, spices, other vegetables, etc.) to make it tastier and more interesting. The analogy suggests that British society is mainly one culture (white and Christian), just like tomato soup is mainly one ingredient (tomato!). But the different cultures, traditions and beliefs that immigrants have brought over the years have added spice and flavour to British society.

So what do you think? Your task here is to explain each analogy in your own words (and think of any new ones if you can!) and explain which one you think best fits British society today. Or, do none of the analogies fit in your opinion? Give reasons for your decision.

TASK 2 'Bloody foreigners'

This is a quote from a best-selling book by Robert Winder called *Bloody Foreigners*, about the impact of immigration on Britain. Here he tries to sum up the 'immigration story'.

'Immigration is a story. And, like all the best stories, it has happy moments as well as sad ones, comedies as well as tragedies. The list of shameful episodes is long, and growing longer every day. But there are uplifting tales too – of people remaking their lives. The immigrant experience is not uniform: some people come hurriedly, as refugees; others to seek their fortunes. Many find heartache, but many have prospered. It has been a momentous adventure both for each individual and for the nation they have settled in and reshaped.'

a From your studies of immigration, can you think of any 'shameful episodes'?

b Can you think of any times when immigrants have 'come hurriedly, as refugees'?

c Can you think of any examples of where people have come to 'seek their fortunes'?

d In what ways have some immigrants found 'heartache' whilst others 'have prospered'?

e List ways in which immigration has 'reshaped' Britain.

TASK 3 So how much do you know? _____

In 2005 the government introduced a computer-based test for any immigrants who wished to become British citizens or settle in Britain for good. The test could be done in test centres around the UK and the questions were based on a book about Britain. The theory behind the test was that anyone wishing to settle in Britain should know about their new country. To pass, candidates needed to get at least 18 (75%) of the 24 questions right.

Below you will find a sample of 12 questions from one of the tests. See how you get on! To pass you'll need to get at least 9 out of 12 (75%) correct.

1. What is the minimum age in the UK to drive a car or motorcycle?
   A 16   B 17   C 18   D 21
2. Which of the following is a public holiday?
   A St Valentine's Day   B Boxing Day
   C April Fool's Day   D The Queen's Birthday
3. When did the Gunpowder Plot take place?
   A 5th November 1505   B 5th November 1605
   C 5th November 1705   D 5th November 1805
4. What is the Wimbledon Championships?
   A Rugby Tournament   B Cricket Tournament
   C Tennis Tournament   D Snooker Tournament
5. What is the highest denomination banknote in England?
   A £100   B £50   C £20   D £10
6. What hours can a child aged 14-16 legally work?
   A Not more than 4 hours without a one hour rest
   B Not more than 5 hours without a one hour rest
   C Not more than 6 hours without a one hour rest
   D Not more than 3 hours without a one hour rest
7. The UK is a member of an international organisation to prevent war and maintain peace. What is it called?
   A United Nations   B Red Cross
   C Save the Children   D FIFA
8. Where does Santa Claus come from?
   A South Pole   B North Pole
   C Poland   D Iceland
9. Which of the following is NOT proof of identity?
   A Recent gas bill   B Passport
   C Home Office Document   D A letter from a close friend
10. The British system of government is a parliamentary democracy.
    A True   B False
11. How much maternity leave can a woman take?
    A 6 weeks   B 10 weeks
    C 13 weeks   D 26 weeks
12. It is illegal to drive a vehicle while using a mobile phone.
    A True   B False

ANSWERS:

1. B	2. B	3. B	4. C
5. B	6. A	7. A	8. B
9. D	10. A	11. D	12. A

Remember, you need at least 9 out of 12 (75%) to pass. Now, why don't you write 12 more questions (with answers) to try on your friends? How much do they know about Britain?

TASK 4 Poetry time _____

This is a poem called 'The British' by Benjamin Zephaniah.

Serves 60 million
Take some Picts, Celts and Silures
And let them settle,
Then overrun them with Roman conquerors.

Remove the Romans after approximately 400 years
Add lots of Norman French to some
Anglos, Saxons, Jutes and Vikings, then stir vigorously.

Mix some hot Chileans, cool Jamaicans, Dominicans,
Trinidadians and Bajans with some Ethiopians, Chinese,
Vietnamese and Sudanese.

Then take a blend of Somalians, Sri Lankans, Nigerians
And Pakistanis,
Combine with some Guyanese
And turn up the heat.

Sprinkle some fresh Indians, Malaysians, Bosnians,
Iraqis and Bangladeshis together with some
Afghans, Spanish, Turkish, Kurdish, Japanese
And Palestinians
Then add to the melting pot.

Leave the ingredients to simmer.

As they mix and blend allow their languages to flourish
Binding them together with English.

Allow time to be cool.

Add some unity, understanding, and respect for the future,
Serve with justice
And enjoy.

Note: All the ingredients are equally important. Treating one ingredient better than another will leave a bitter unpleasant taste.

Warning: An unequal spread of justice will damage the people and cause pain. Give justice and equality to all.

a List all the different countries and places mentioned in the poem where people have come from over the years to make up 'The British'.

b The poem attempts to get across the views of the poet. What do you think the poem's messages are?

c In your opinion, has the poet communicated these messages well?

d Find out about the poet – his background, beliefs and other work he has done.

Glossary

Anglo-Irish Agreement cause people to feel isolated or unwelcome

asylum seeker – someone who flees to another country to escape danger in their own country

ayahs – children's nannies in India

Beaker People – Bronze Age settlers arriving in England

British Nationality Act – passed in 1948, this act allowed anyone living in the British Empire (the Commonwealth) to live and work in Britain

Bronze Age – a period of time after the Stone Age, during which people began to make weapons and tools out of bronze (a mixture of tin and copper), rather than stone and wood

civil rights – the rights of citizens to political and social freedom and equality

Commonwealth – the countries in the British Empire

community cohesion – togetherness and bonding between the people in a community

dialects – varieties of language that are only found in a particular area of a country

divisive – causing disagreements between people

economic migrants – people who come to a new country in order to find work

emigrants – people who move out of a country

ethnic minority – a group of people of a different race or culture from the majority race or culture in the country where they live

European Union (EU) – an association of several European countries. Anyone from one EU country can live and work in any other EU country

fascists – people believing in a system of government run by a dictator, often with policies of nationalism and racism

forced migration – when people have little or no choice but to leave the country in which they live

Huguenots – French Catholics in the 1600s and 1700s

hunter-gatherers – people in the Stone Age period who lived by gathering food such as fruit and nuts and by killing animals for meat and furs.

illegal immigration – coming to live in a country illegally, for example, by being smuggled, without any proper documentation

immigration – coming to live in a new country

India – a country in South Asia. At the time of the British Empire, all the countries in South Asia (including India, Pakistan, Bangladesh, Sri Lanka and Burma) were called India by the British

interest – a fee charged by money lenders for giving someone a loan

interned – confined as a prisoner

lascars – South Asian sailors

member states – countries or states belonging to the European Union (EU)

migrant – a person who moves to another country

migration – the movement of people between countries

MORI poll – a type of social or political survey

multicultural – several different cultural groups within a society

net migration – the final change in population in a country after everyone leaving and everyone moving in have been taken into account

pagans – people who are not Christian, Jewish or Muslim, and believe in lots of different gods

parody – an exaggerated imitation of something

persecution – people being abused and treated cruelly

pneumonia – a lung infection

pogroms – organised killings of a particular group or race of people

refugees – people who have been forced to leave their country to escape war, persecution or natural disaster

stereotypical – fixed, generalised ideas about how a group of people would behave

Stone Age – a period of time before the Bronze Age, during which weapons and tools were made mostly of stone

visa – documentation giving permission to stay in a country

voluntary migration – when people choose to move countries

Index

EASY CROCHET: HATS

EASY CROCHET: HATS

MARGARET HUBERT

APPLE

For my wonderful grandchildren, the sunshine of my life.

Acknowledgments

I wish to thank Alchemy Yarns of Transformation, Berroco, Inc., Lion Brand Yarn Company, Patons Yarns, Plymouth Yarn Company, and Tahki/Stacy Charles, Inc., who so graciously donated yarns for most of the projects in this book. I also wish to thank Jeannine Buehler for helping me crochet some of the hats.

First published by Apple Press in 2006

Sheridan House
114 Western Road
Hove, East Sussex, BN3 1DD, UK
www.apple-press.com

ISBN-10: 1-84543-132-4
ISBN 13: 978-84543-132-7

Created and produced by
Creative Publishing international
18705 Lake Drive East
Chanhassen, MN 55317
U.S.A.
www.creativepub.com

Printed in China

10 9 8 7 6 5 4 3 2 1

Visit the following web sites for more information about the yarns shown in this book:

Alchemy Yarns of Transformation
www.alchemyyarns.com

Berroco, Inc.
www.berrocco.com

Brown Sheep Company, Inc.
www.brownsheep.com

Caron International
www.caron.com

Katia Yarns/Knitting Fever
www.knittingfever.com

Lion Brand Yarn Company
www.lionbrand.com

On Line Yarns/Knitting Fever
www.knittingfever.com

Patons Yarns
www.patonsyarns.com

Plymouth Yarn Company
www.plymouthyarn.com

Sirdar Spinning Company
www.sirdar.co.uk

Tahki/Stacy Charles, Inc.
www.tahkistacycharles.com

Wool Pak Yarns NZ
www.baabajoeswool.com

Contents

About the Projects

A crocheted hat can be a hip beanie that a teen wears everywhere, or a pastel baby hat with a curlicue on top. It can be a big-brimmed hat for summer or a furry hood for the coldest day of winter. It can be super-bulky or lacey mesh, pretty or sophisticated. You will find all these kinds of hooked hats and many more in *Easy Crochet: Hats.*

I have designed twenty hats that are all fun, fast, and in fashion. All are easy, even if you are a beginner. Several hats are made using only single crochet. A multi-textured, multi-coloured yarn can turn the most basic, single-crochet hat into a work of art! Other hats feature textural stitches that are easy to learn.

Some hats are worked in the round, beginning at the crown and working down to the brim. Other hats are crocheted in rows and sewn together in the back. If you need to learn or review a stitch, just go to the basics section at the back, which has detailed, photographed instructions.

For each hat, I chose a yarn to complement the stitch and the style of the hat. Smooth cotton yarns are great for warm-weather hats and caps. They show off the texture of the crochet stitches and are good for decorative stitches like shells or popcorn, and they make even single crochet look fascinating. Hats made with cotton yarns also wear and wash well. For the Silky Cloche, I used a beautiful smooth silk yarn that shimmers in the light. Highly textured novelty yarns give a hat special character, but the stitches don't show, so I use simple stitches and let the yarn take centre stage. For the Hot Textures Hat, a lovely ribbon yarn is combined with a highly textured acrylic yarn in a single crochet ribbing pattern to make it not only fun and interesting but also warm.

The wonderful new yarns offer many choices. You can make a hat lightweight and airy or warm and wooly, thick or thin, in natural colours or all the colours of the rainbow.

Give your hats personality by adding a flower or two or a special hatband. Tassels on earflaps, corkscrews on crowns, pom-poms on ties—mix and match elements.

The materials lists will tell you the weight and type of each yarn, as well as the brands and colours I used. You can substitute different yarns of the same weight and certainly choose your own colours.

While most crocheted hats have some "give" and will fit several sizes, it is still necessary to measure your head and check your gauge to ensure a good fit. For an accurate head measurement, place a tape measure across the forehead and, holding the tape snugly, measure around the full circumference of the head. Crochet a sample with your yarn and the hook size suggested to make sure your gauge matches the gauge listed. If you do not get the proper gauge, try a larger or smaller hook. You can also change the hook size to make a particular hat a little smaller or larger.

If you are new to crochet, I hope this book will help you learn the stitches and inspire you to hook one hat after another. If you are already hooked on crochet, I hope that you will enjoy my ideas and patterns. Enjoy watching each hat take shape and become a thing of beauty that you will be proud to wear or give.

Margaret Hubert is also the author of Hooked Bags, Hooked Throws, Hooked Scarves, How to Free-Form Crochet *and six other books. She designs crochet projects for yarn companies and magazines and teaches at yarn shops, retreats and national gatherings.*

Silky Cloche

This is a classic cloche to wear spring through fall.

You can wear the brim down or flipped up on the

front, side or all around. Add flair with a bright

flower or a hatband if you like (see Hat

Embellishments on page 26).

(see Hat Embellishments on page 26)

YARN

Lightweight silk/wool
blend yarn

Shown: Synchronicity by
Alchemy, 50% silk 50% merino
wool, 1.75 oz (50 g)/110 yd
(101 m): Bronze #090M,
3 skeins

HOOKS

9/I (5.5 mm)
8/H (5 mm)

STITCH USED

Single crochet

GAUGE

$3\frac{1}{2}$ sc = 1" (2.5 cm)
on 9/I hook

NOTIONS

Stitch marker
Tapestry needle

FINISHED SIZE

20" to 22" (51 to 56 cm)
head circumference

9

Lightweight silk/wool blend yarn in single crochet.

HAT

Hat is worked with double strand throughout.

Foundation rnd: Using 9/I hook, ch 4, join with Sl st to form ring.

Rnd 1: Work 8 sc in ring, pm for beg of rnds, carry marker up at end of each rnd.

Rnd 2: Work 2 sc in each st around (16 sc).

Rnd 3: * Work 1 sc in next st, 2 sc in next st, rep from * around (24 sc).

Rnd 4: * Work 1 sc in each of next 2 sts, 2 sc in next st, rep from * around (32 sc).

Rnd 5: * Work 1 sc in each of next 3 sts, 2 sc in next st, rep from * around (40 sc).

Rnd 6: * Work 1 sc in each of next 4 sts, 2 sc in next st, rep from * around (48 sc).

Rnd 7: * Work 1 sc in each of next 5 sts, 2 sc in next st, rep from * around (56 sc).

Rnd 8: * Work 1 sc in each of next 6 sts, 2 sc in next st, rep from * around (64 sc).

Rnds 9–18: Work even.

Rnd 19 (first inc rnd): * Work 1 sc in each of next 3 sts, 2 sc in next st, rep from * around, end 2 sc in last st (80 sc).

Rnds 20–28: Work even.

Rnds 29–32: Change to 8/H hook. Work even.

Rnd 33 (second inc rnd): Change back to 9/I hook. * Work 1 sc in each of next 9 sts, 2 sc in next st, rep from * around (90 sc).

Rnds 34–41: Work even, end last rnd with Sl st, fasten off, weave in ends using tapestry needle.

Hot Textures Hat

Chunky, stylish hats are easy to make with today's

textural yarns. This hat has twice the texture, since it's

made with a smooth ribbon yarn and a nubby acrylic

yarn hooked together. For even more surface interest,

the pattern creates a ribbed effect by working single

crochet stitches through the back loop on every row.

YARN

Bulky-weight ribbon yarn

Shown: Incredible by Lion Brand, 100% nylon, 1.75 oz (50 g)/110 yd (100 m): Purple Party #207, 2 balls

Bulky-weight acrylic yarn

Shown: Homespun by Lion Brand, 98% acrylic/2% polyester, 6 oz (170 g)/185 yd (170 m): Coral Gables #370, 1 skein

HOOK

10½/K (6.5 mm)

STITCHES USED

Single crochet

Single crochet through back loop

GAUGE

10 sc = 4" (10 cm)

NOTION

Tapestry needle

FINISHED SIZE

20" to 22" (51 to 56 cm) head circumference

13

Ribbed effect created by working single crochet through back loops.

HAT

Hat is worked with one strand of each yarn held together throughout.

Foundation row: Ch 45. Starting in second ch from hook, work 1 sc in each ch to end, ch 1, turn.

Row 1: Sk first st, * work 1 sc tbl in next st, rep from * across, work 1 sc in tch, ch 1, turn (44 sc). Rep row 1 for 9" (23 cm).

Begin crown shaping as follows:

Row 1: Sk first st, work 1 sc in next st * sc2tog, sc in next st, sc in next st, rep from * across (33 sc), ch 1, turn.

Row 2: Sk first st, * work 1 sc tbl in next st, rep from * across, work 1 sc in tch, ch 1, turn.

Row 3: Sk first st, sc2tog, * work 1 sc in next st, sc2tog, rep from * across, making last sc in tch (22 sc), ch 1, turn.

Rows 4 and 5: Rep row 2 of crown shaping.

Row 6: Sk first st, * sc2tog, rep from * across, end 1 sc (11 sc), fasten off, leaving long tail.

Ribbon yarn in reverse single crochet accents the brim edge.

FINISHING

1. With right side of brim facing, using ribbon yarn only, work one row of single crochet along edge, do not turn. Work one row of reverse single crochet across row, fasten off.

2. Thread the yarn tail onto a tapestry needle. Gather the remaining stitches at the top, but don't cut the yarn.

3. Sew the back seam and weave in ends.

Poodle Cap

This cuddly, head-hugging cap is made

with a novelty bouclé yarn. Made

entirely in single crochet, this is a

great project for beginners.

Super bulky bouclé yarn in single crochet.

YARN

Super bulky bouclé yarn

Shown: Pooch by Patons, 63% acrylic/27% wool/10% nylon, 2.4 oz (68 g)/36 yd (33 m): Indian Summer #65610, 1 ball

HOOK

10 1/2 /K (6.5 mm)

STITCH USED

Single crochet

GAUGE

6 1/2 sc = 4" (10 cm)

NOTIONS

Stitch marker

Tapestry needle

FINISHED SIZE

20" to 21" (51 to 53.5 cm) head circumference

CAP

Foundation rnd: Ch 4, join with Sl st to form ring. Work 6 sc in center of ring, pm for beg of rnds, carry marker up at end of each rnd, do not join with Sl st after each rnd.

Rnd 1: Work 2 sc in each st (12 sc).

Rnd 2: * Work 1 sc in next st, 2 sc in next st, rep from * around (18 sc).

Rnd 3: * Work 1 sc in each of next 2 sts, 2 sc in next st, rep from * around (24 sc).

Rnd 4: * Work 1 sc in each of next 3 sts, 2 sc in next st, rep from * around (30 sc).

Rnd 5: * Work 1 sc in each of next 4 sts, 2 sc in next st, rep from * around (36 sc).

Rnds 6–11: Work 1 sc in each st around, fasten off, leaving a 4" (10 cm) length of yarn, weave in ends using tapestry needle.

Chenille Cloche

Chenille yarns are so soft and cozy. This cloche

has drama. You can add a crescent

embellishment (see page 26).

YARN

Super bulky weight
chenille yarn

Shown: Chenille Thick & Quick
by Lion Brand, 91% acrylic/9%
rayon, 100 yd (92 m): Grass
Green #130, 1 skein

HOOK

10½/K (6.5 mm)

STITCHES USED

Single crochet

Half double crochet

GAUGE

8 sc = 4" (10 cm)

NOTION

Tapestry needle

FINISHED SIZE

20" to 21" (51 to 53.5 cm)
head circumference

Chenille yarn in alternating rows of single crochet and half double crochet.

HAT

Foundation row: Ch 43. Starting in second ch from hook, work 1 sc in each ch to end, ch 2, turn.

Row 1: Sk first st (tch counts as first st now and throughout), * work 1 hdc in next st, rep from * across (42 hdc), ch 1, turn.

Row 2: Sk first st, * work 1 sc in next st, rep from * across (42 sc), ch 2, turn.

Rep rows 1 and 2 for 7" (18 cm) from beg, ending with sc row, ch 1, turn.

Crown of hat is worked entirely in sc.

First dec row: * Work 1 sc in each of next 12 sts, sc2tog, rep from * 2 times more (39 sc), ch 1, turn.

Second dec row: * Work 1 sc in each of next 7 sts, sc2tog, rep from * 3 times more, 1 sc, 1 sc in top of tch (35 sc), ch 1, turn.

Third dec row: Work 1 sc in each of next 2 sts, sc2tog, * sc in each of next 3 sts, sc2tog, rep from * 5 times (28 sc), ch 1, turn.

Work 1 row even, ch 1, turn.

Fourth dec row: * Work 1 sc in each of next 2 sts, sc2tog, rep from * (21 sc), ch 1, turn.

Work 1 row even, ch 1, turn.

Fifth dec row: * Work 1 sc in next st, sc2tog, rep from * (14 sc), ch 1, turn.

Work 1 row even, ch 1, turn.

Sixth dec row: Sc2tog across, fasten off, leaving long tail for sewing.

FINISHING

1. Thread the yarn tail onto a tapestry needle. Gather the remaining stitches at the top, but don't cut the yarn.
2. Sew the back seam and weave in ends.
3. Embellish with a spiral crescent (page 26), if desired.

Peach Cooler

This is a fresh style for spring and summer. The brim can be folded up or rolled. It will hold its shape because it is crocheted with two strands of cotton.

YARN

Lightweight cotton yarn in two colours

Shown: Cotton Classic by Tahki/Stacy Charles, 100% cotton, 1.75 oz (50 g)/108 yd (100 m): Dark Peach #3473, 2 skeins; Light Peach #3476, 2 skeins

HOOKS

9/I (5.5 mm)

6/G (4 mm)

STITCH USED

Single crochet

GAUGE

14 sc = 4" (10 cm) on 9/I hook

NOTIONS

Stitch marker

Tapestry needle

FINISHED SIZE

20" to 21" (51 to 53.5 cm) head circumference

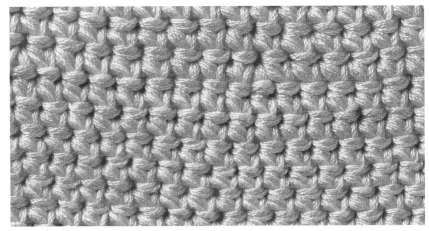

Two strands of lightweight cotton yarn in slightly different shades worked together in single crochet.

HAT

Hat is worked with one strand of each yarn held tog throughout. WS of sc is used as RS of hat.

Foundation rnd: Using 9/I hook, ch 4, join with Sl st to form ring. Work 8 sc in ring, pm after eighth st, do not join, do not ch, carry marker up at end of each rnd.

Rnd 1: * Work 2 sc in next st, rep from * around (16 sc).

Rnd 2: * Work 1 sc in next st, 2 sc in next st, rep from * around (24 sc).

Rnd 3: * Work 1 sc in each of next 2 sts, 2 sc in next st, rep from * around (32 sc).

Rnd 4: * Work 1 sc in each of next 3 sts, 2 sc in next st, rep from * around (40 sc).

Rnd 5: * Work 1 sc in each of next 4 sts, 2 sc in next st, rep from * around (48 sc).

Rnds 6 and 7: * Work 1 sc in next st, rep from * around (48 sc).

Rnd 8: * Work 1 sc in each of next 5 sts, 2 sc in next st, rep from * around (56 sc).

Rnds 9 and 10: Rep rnds 6 and 7.

Rows of tight single crochet stitches cause the hat brim to roll.

Rnd 11: * Work 1 sc in each of next 6 sts, 2 sc in next st, rep from * around (64 sc).

Rnds 12 and 13: Rep rnds 6 and 7.

Rnd 14: * Work 1 sc in each of next 7 sts, 2 sc in next st, rep from * around (72 sc).

Rnds 15–28: Rep rnd 6, join with Sl st, and turn, reversing direction.

Start brim as follows:

Rnd 29 (first inc row): * Work 1 sc in each of next 17 sts, 2 sc in next st, rep from * around (76 sc).

Rnd 30: Rep rnd 6.

Rnd 31 (second inc row): Work 1 sc in each of next 2 sts, * 1 sc in each of next 7 sts, 2 sc in next st, rep from * around, end sc in each of last 2 sts (85 sc).

Rnd 32: Rep rnd 6.

Rnd 33 (third inc row): Work 1 sc in next st, * 1 sc in each of next 6 sts, 2 sc in next st, rep from * around (99 sc).

Rnd 34: Change to 6/G hook. Rep rnd 6 (this tightens brim, causing it to roll up), fasten off, weave in ends using tapestry needle.

Hat Embellishments

You can dress up your hats with crocheted embellishments in contrasting colours and textures. Add a scalloped hatband to any of the cloches. Crochet a flower or a wavy crescent to accent any of the close-fitting caps, cloches or brimmed hats. Sew the flourishes in place or use safety pins for quick changes.

HATBAND

Hatband is worked with double strand throughout.

Foundation rnd: Using 9/I hook, ch 5, join with Sl st to form ring.

Work 6 hdc, ch 4, 1 hdc in ring. * Turn, ch 1, work 6 hdc, ch 4, 1 hdc in ch-4 sp. Rep from * until hatband is 22" (56 cm), fasten off, weave in ends using tapestry needle.

Using tapestry needle, sew ends tog. Attach hatband to hat.

CRESCENT

Foundation row: Using 10½/K hook, ch 14.

Row 1: Starting in 3rd ch from hook, work 1 hdc in each ch to end, turn.

Row 2: Ch 3, * work 3 dc in each st to end, fasten off, leaving a long tail for sewing.

Twist crescent into floral shape, sew together using tapestry needle, and weave in ends. Attach crescent to hat.

ROSE

Foundation rnd: Using 5/F hook, ch 4, join with Sl st to form ring.

Rnd 1: Work 12 sc in ring, join with Sl st to first sc, ch 1.

Rnd 2: Sc in same sc, * ch 3, sk 1, sc in next sc, rep from * around, end ch 3, sk 1 sc, and join in first st (7 lps).

Rnd 3: * In next ch lp, work [sc, hdc, 3 dc, hdc, sc], rep from * around, end Sl st in first sc, fasten off.

Rnd 4: Working in back of petals (in the skipped sc), join yarn in BL of sc on the second rnd below last and first petals, * ch 5, sc tbl of next sc on second rnd below next 2 petals, rep from * around, end ch 5, sc in joining st.

Rnd 5: In next ch lp, work [sc, hdc, 5 dc, hdc, sc], rep from * around, end Sl st in first sc, fasten off, weave in ends using tapestry needle. Attach rose to hat.

HAT EMBELLISHMENTS

YARN

Hatband: Lightweight silk/wool blend yarn

Shown: Synchronicity by Alchemy, 50% silk/50% merino wool, 1.75 oz (50 g)/110 yd (101 m): Bronze #090M, 3 skeins

Crescent: Super bulky weight chenille yarn

Shown: Chenille Thick & Quick by Lion Brand, 91% acrylic/9% rayon, 100 yd (92 m): Grass Green #130, 1 skein

Rose: Medium weight ribbon yarn

Shown: Berroco Glacé, 100% rayon, 1.75 oz (50 g)/75 yd (69 m): Shock #2518

HOOKS

Hatband: 9/I (5.5 mm)

Crescent: 10½/K (6.5 mm)

Rose: 5/F (3.75 mm)

STITCHES USED

Single crochet

Single crochet through back loop

Double crochet

Half double crochet

GAUGE

Varies with yarn and hook

NOTION

Tapestry needle

FINISHED SIZES

Hatband: 22" (56 cm)

Crescent: 3" (7.5 cm)

Rose: 3" (7.5 cm)

Mesh Cap

An open-work mesh cap has lots of attitude. If you

love this downtown look, crochet it in lots of colours

including natural cotton.

YARN

Medium-weight cotton/rayon blend yarn

Shown: Cotton Twist by Berroco, 70% cotton/30% rayon, 1.75 oz (50 g)/85 yd (78 m): Crème Fraiche #8374, 1 skein

HOOK

6/G (4 mm)

STITCHES USED

Single crochet

Double crochet

Reverse single crochet

GAUGE

7 dc, 6 ch-2 sp = 4" (10 cm)

NOTION

Tapestry needle

FINISHED SIZE

20" to 21" (51 to 53.5 cm) head circumference

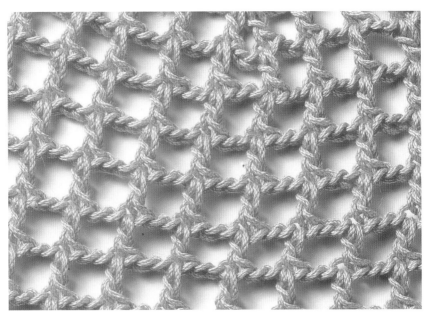

Double crochet and chain stitches form open-work mesh.

Foundation rnd: Ch 4, join with Sl st to form ring. Ch 4, (counts as dc, ch 1), work [dc, ch 1] in ring 7 times (8 dc), join with Sl st to third ch of beg ch 4.

Rnd 1: Ch 5 (counts as 1 dc, ch 2, now and throughout), work 1 dc in same st, ch 2, * [1 dc, ch 2, 1 dc] in next st (inc made), ch 2, rep from * around, join with Sl st to third ch of beg ch 5 (16 dc).

Rnd 2: Ch 5, work 1 dc in same st, ch 2, 1 dc in next st, ch 2, * [1 dc, ch 2, 1 dc] in next st (inc made), ch 2, 1 dc next st, ch 2, rep from * around, join with Sl st to third ch of beg ch 5 (24 dc).

Rnd 3: Ch 5, work 1 dc in same st, ch 2, 1 dc in next st, ch 2, 1 dc in next st, ch 2, * [1 dc, ch 2, 1 dc] in next st (inc made), ch 2, 1 dc in next st, ch 2, 1 dc in next st, ch 2, rep from * around, join with Sl st to third ch of beg ch 5 (32 dc).

Rnd 4: Ch 5, * work 1 dc in next st, ch 2, rep from * around, join with Sl st to third ch of beg ch 5.

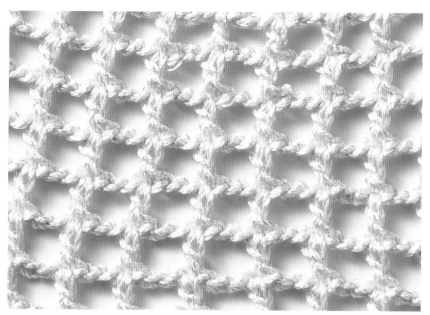

Shown in a natural colour. The rayon fibers in the blended yarn have a soft luster.

Rnds 5–15: Rep rnd 4.

Rnd 16: Ch 1, * work 2 sc in next ch-2 sp, rep from * around, join with Sl st to beg ch 1.

Rnd 17: Work rev sc back over all sts of rnd 16, fasten off, weave in ends using tapestry needle.

Summer Breeze Brimmed Hat

Sometimes it's all about the stitch. This hat is all about the shell stitch. Crocheted with two strands of yarn throughout to give it body, this hat has a slight brim to keep the sun off your face.

YARN

Medium-weight cotton/rayon blend yarn

Shown: Cotton Twist by Berroco, 70% cotton/30% rayon, 1.75 oz (50 g)/85 yd (78 m): Corot #8339, 4 skeins

HOOKS

6/G (4 mm)

8/H (5 mm)

STITCHES USED

Single crochet

Single crochet through back loop

Double crochet

Shell stitch

GAUGE

3 shell clusters = 4" (10 cm) on 6/G hook

2 shell clusters = 4" (10 cm) on 8/H hook

NOTIONS

Stitch marker

Tapestry needle

FINISHED SIZE

20" to 21" (51 to 53.5 cm) head circumference

Clusters of double crochet stitches form asymetrical shells.

HAT

Yarn is used double strand throughout.

Foundation rnd: Using 6/G hook, ch 4, join with Sl st to form ring. Work 8 sc in ring, pm for beg of rnds, carry marker up at end of each rnd.

Rnd 1: * Work 2 sc in next st, rep from * around (16 sc).

Rnd 2: * Work 1 sc in next st, 2 sc in next st, rep from * around (24 sc).

Rnd 3: * Work 1 sc in each of next 2 sts, 2 sc in next st, rep from * around (32 sc).

Rnd 4: * Work 1 sc in each of next 3 sts, 2 sc in next st, rep from * around (40 sc).

Rnd 5: * Work 1 sc in each of next 4 sts, 2 sc in next st, rep from * around (48 sc).

Rnd 6: * Work 1 sc in each of next 5 sts, 2 sc in next st, rep from * around (56 sc).

Rnd 7: * Work 1 sc in each of next 6 sts, 2 sc in next st, rep from * around (64 sc).

Rnd 8: * Work 1 sc in each of next 7 sts, 2 sc in next st, rep from * around (72 sc), join with Sl st, cont carry marker up after each rnd. Begin asymmetrical shell pattern as follows:

Rnd 9: Ch 3, sk 3 sts, * work [4 dc, ch 2, 1 dc] in next st, sk 4 sts, rep from * 13 times, join with Sl st to top of beg ch 3 (14 shell sts), ch 3, turn.

Rnd 10: * Work [4 dc, ch 2, 1 dc] in next ch-2 sp, rep from * 13 times, join with Sl st to top of of beg ch 3 (14 shell sts), ch 3, turn.

Rnds 11 and 12: Rep rnd 10, at end on rnd 12, ch 1 instead of 3, turn.

Rnd 13: Work 2 sc in first ch-2 sp, * 1 sc in each of next 4 sts, 1 sc in next ch-2 sp, rep from * around (72 sc), do not join, do not turn, cont carry marker.

Rnds 14 and 15: Sc tbl in each st around. At end of rnd 15, join with Sl st to first st of rnd, do not turn.

Rnd 16: Rep rnd 9.

Rnd 17: Rep rnd 10.

Rnd 18: Change to 8/H hook. Rep rnd 10, do not turn.

Rnd 19: * Work 1 sc in each of next 4 sts, 2 sc in ch-2 sp, rep from * around (84 sc).

Rnds 20 and 21: Sc tbl in each st around.

Rnd 22: Rep rnd 9 (16 shells).

Rnd 23: Rep rnd 10, end ch 1 instead of 3, turn.

Rnd 24: * Work 1 sc in each of next 4 sts, 2 sc in ch-2 sp, rep from * around, join with Sl st to beg ch 1, fasten off, weave in ends using tapestry needle.

Weaving Ribbon Cloche

Bright contrasting colours really pop. This is a low-fitting cloche with a row of eyelets that holds a crocheted ribbon. Change the ribbon to change the look. You can even make a ribbon out of a fun fur yarn.

YARN

Medium-weight cotton yarn for hat

Shown: Cotton Classic II by Tahki/Stacy Charles, 100% cotton, 1.75 oz (50 g)/ 74 yd (68 m): #2924, 2 skeins

Lightweight cotton yarn for ribbon

Shown: Cotton Classic by Tahki/Stacy Charles, 100% cotton, 1.75 oz (50 g)/108 yd (100 m): #3760, 1 skein

HOOKS

10½/K (6.5 mm) for hat

9/I (5.5 mm) for ribbon

STITCHES USED

Single crochet

Double crochet

GAUGE

8 dc = 4" (10 cm) on 10½/K hook

NOTION

Tapestry needle

FINISHED SIZE

20" to 21" (51 to 53.5 cm) head circumference

Two strands of medium-weight cotton yarn in double crochet.

HAT

Yarn is used double strand throughout.

Foundation rnd: Using 10½/K hook, ch 4, join with SI st to form ring. Work 9 sc in ring, join with SI st.

Rnd 1: Ch 3 (counts as dc now and throughout), work 1 dc in same st as ch 3, 2 dc in each sc around (18 dc), join with SI st to top of beg ch 3.

Rnd 2: Ch 3, sk first st, * work 2 dc in next st, 1 dc in next st, rep from * around, 2 dc in same st as beg ch 3 (27 dc), join with SI st to top of beg ch 3.

Rnd 3: Ch 3, sk first st, work 1 dc in next st, * 2 dc in next st, 1 dc in each of next 2 sts, rep from * 7 times, 2 dc in same st as beg ch 3 (36 dc), join with SI st to top of beg ch 3.

Rnd 4: Ch 3, sk first st, work 1 dc in next 2 sts, * 2 dc in next st, 1 dc in each of next 3 sts, rep from * 7 times, 2 dc in same st as beg ch 3 (45 dc), join with SI st to top of beg ch 3.

Rnd 5: Ch 3, sk first st, work 1 dc in each st around, 1 dc in same st as beg ch 3 (45 dc), join with SI st to top of beg ch 3.

Rep rnd 5 for 6½" (16.3 cm) from beg.

Open-work rnd: Ch 4 (counts as 1 dc, ch 1), sk st that ch 3 is coming from, sk next st, work 1 dc in next st, * ch 1, sk 1, 1 dc in next st, rep from * around, join with SI st to third ch of beg ch 4, ch 1.

Open-work round creates holes for weaving ribbon.

Begin brim as follows:

Rnd 1: * Work 1 sc in ch-1 sp, 1 sc in next st, rep from * around (45 sc), join with Sl st to beg ch 1, ch 1.

Rnd 2: Sk first st, work 1 sc in each st around, join with Sl st to beg ch 1, ch 1.

Rnd 3: Sk first st, work 1 sc in each of next 7 sts, 2 sc in next st (inc made), * sc in each of next 8 sts, inc in next st, rep from * around (50 sc), join with Sl st to beg ch 1, ch 1.

Rnd 4: Sk first st, work 1 sc in each of next 8 sts, inc in next st, * sc in each of next 9 sts, inc in next st, rep from * around (55 sc), join with Sl st to beg ch 1, ch 1.

Rnd 5: Sk first st, work 1 sc in each of next 9 sts, inc in next st, * sc in each of next 10 sts, inc in next st, rep from * around (60 sc), fasten off, weave in ends using tapestry needle.

RIBBON
Foundation row: Using 9/I hook and 1 strand of lightweight yarn, ch 5. Starting in second ch from hook, work 1 sc in each ch, ch 1, turn.

Row 1: Sk first st, 1 sc in each st to end, ch 1, turn.

Rep row 1 for 36" (91.5 cm), fasten off, weave in ends using tapestry needle.

FINISHING
Weave ribbon in and out of open-work row, overlap and tie ends.

New Plaid Tam

Everyone is mad about plaid, and a jaunty tam is

the ultimate plaid accessory. Did you know you

could make plaid with crochet? The raised bars on

this hat are made with front post double crochet.

Don't be intimidated; you'll pick up the pattern

quickly once you start.

YARN

Medium-weight acrylic yarn

Shown: Simply Soft Brites by Caron, 100% acrylic, 6 oz (170 g)/315 yd (290 m): Blue Mint #9608, 1 skein (MC)

Bulky-weight ribbon yarn

Shown: On Line Linie, 100% polyacrylic, 1.75 oz (50 g)/100 yd (92 m): Space #114, 1 skein (CC)

HOOKS

6/G (4 mm)

9/I (5.5 mm)

10/J (6 mm)

STITCHES USED

Single crochet

Half double crochet

Front post double crochet

Reverse single crochet

GAUGE

16 sc = 4" (10 cm) on 6/G hook

14 hdc = 4" (10 cm) on 9/I hook

11 hdc = 4" (10 cm) on 10/J hook

NOTIONS

Stitch marker

Tapestry needle

8" (20.5 cm) piece of cardboard

FINISHED SIZE

20" (51 cm) head circumference

Ribbon yarn in single crochet forms raised bars in the plaid design.

HAT

Foundation rnd: Using 6/G hook and MC, starting with band, ch 76. Being careful not to twist, join with Sl st to form ring. Using a CC yarn, pm.

Rnd 1: Sc in each ch around, carry up marker now and at end of every rnd of band.

Rnd 2: Sc in each st around.

Rnds 3, 4, and 5: Rep rnd 2.

Rnd 6: Work 1 sc in first st, 2 sc in next st (inc made), * sc in each of next 8 sts, inc in next st, rep from * 7 times more, sc in each of last 2 sts (85 sc). End of band.

Change to 9/I hook and begin crown as follows:

Rnd 1: Ch 2 (counts as first hdc now and throughout), work 1 hdc in each st around (85 hdc), join with Sl st to top of beg ch 2.

Rnd 2: Ch 2, work 1 hdc in each of next 5 sts, * 1 FPdc over next hdc, 1 hdc in next st, 1 FPdc over next hdc, 1 hdc in each of next 11 sts, rep from * 4 times more, 1 FPdc over next hdc, 1 hdc in next st, 1 FPdc over next hdc, 1 hdc in each of next 6 sts, join with Sl st to top of beg ch 2, join CC, ch 2 (at end of this rnd, there will be 6 hdc at beg, 6 raised ribs with 11 hdc bet, 6 hdc at end).

Rnd 3: With CC, rep rnd 2, ch 2 with MC.

Rnds 4–7: Change to 10/J hook. With MC, rep rnd 2. At end of rnd 7, ch 2 with CC.

Rnd 8: With CC, rep rnd 2, ch 2 with MC.

Rnd 9 (first dec row): With MC, ch 2, work 1 hdc in each of next 3 sts, dec over next 2 sts (to dec, hdc, yo pick up lp in next st, yo pick up lp in next st, yo through all 5 lps on hook), * 1 FPdc over next FPdc, 1 hdc next st, 1 FPdc over next FPdc, dec over next 2 sts, 1 hdc in each of next 7 sts, dec over next 2 sts, rep from * 4 times, 1 FPdc, 1 hdc, 1 FPdc, dec over next 2 sts, 1 hdc in each of rem 4 sts, join with Sl st to top of beg ch 2 (73 sts).

Rnd 10: With MC, foll patt as established.

Rnd 11 (second dec row): With MC, dec 1 st before and after each raised rib (61 sts).

Rnd 12: With MC, foll patt as established.

Rnd 13 (3rd dec row): With CC, dec 1 st before and after each raised rib (49 sts).

Rnd 14: With MC, foll patt as established.

Rnd 15 (4th dec row): With MC, dec 1 st before and after each raised rib (37 sts).

Rnd 16: With MC, foll patt as established.

Rnd 17 (5th dec row): With MC, ch 2, work 1 FPdc, 1 hdc, 1 FPdc, * dec over next 2 sts , 1 hdc, 1 FPdc, 1 hdc, 1 FPdc, rep from * ending with Sl st to top of beg ch 2.

Rnd 18: With CC, ch 2, foll patt as established.

Rnd 19: With MC, ch 2, * work 1 FPdc, 1 hdc, 1 FPdc, 1 hdc, rep from * ending with Sl st in top of beg ch 2.

Rnd 20: With MC, ch 2, * work 1 FPdc, sk hdc, rep from * ending with Sl st in top of beg ch 2, fasten off, leaving an 18" (46 cm) end.

FINISHING

1. Using tapestry needle, draw long end through top of last row and pull up tight, knot, fasten off, weave in ends.
2. With CC and 9/I hook, work sc from top to bottom over each row of FPdc, forming vertical rows of plaid, weave in ends.
3. With MC and 6/G hook, work 1 row of sc and 1 row of rev sc around bottom of band, weave in ends.
4. To create tassel, wrap ribbon around an 8" (20.5 cm) piece of cardboard about 15 times. Thread a piece of ribbon under the loops at the top and tie tightly. Slip the loops off the cardboard. Tie another piece of ribbon around the loops 1" (2.5 cm) down from the top. Cut the loops at the other end. Tie the tassel to the cap point.

Simple Stuff Beanie

Beanies are on snowboarders, skateboarders and lots of other teens and twenties who just like the look. Here is the first of three styles of this simple, close-fitting cap, which is sometimes called a skullcap or a bicycle hat. This first style has narrow stripes.

YARN

Medium-weight acrylic yarn

Shown: Canadiana by Patons, 100% acrylic, 3.5 oz (100g)/201 yd (185 m): Denim #00303, 1 skein (MC); Stonewash #00305, 1 skein (CC)

HOOK

9/I (5.5 mm)

STITCHES USED

Single crochet

Double crochet

GAUGE

12 dc = 4" (10 cm)

NOTION

Tapestry needle

FINISHED SIZE

20" to 22" (51 to 56 cm) head circumference

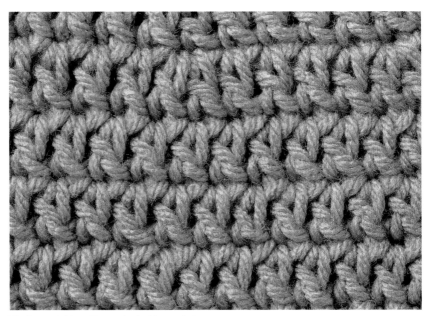

Medium-weight acrylic yarn in double crochet.

CAP

Foundation rnd: With MC, ch 4, join with SI st to form ring.

Rnd 1: Ch 3 (counts as dc now and throughout), work 9 dc in ring, join with SI st to top of beg ch 3.

Rnd 2: Ch 3, work 1 dc in same st as ch 3, 2 dc in each rem st around, join with SI st to top of beg ch 3 (20 dc).

Rnd 3: Ch 3, work 2 dc in next st, * 1 dc in next st, 2 dc in next st, rep from * around, join with SI st to top of beg ch 3 (30 dc).

Rnd 4: Ch 3, work 1 dc in next st, 2 dc in next st, * 1 dc in each of next 2 sts, 2 dc in next st, rep from * around, join with SI st to top of beg ch 3 (40 dc).

Rnd 5: Ch 3, work 1 dc in each of next 2 sts, 2 dc in next st, * 1 dc in each of next 3 sts, 2 dc in next st, rep from * around, join with SI st to top of beg ch 3 (50 dc).

Rnd 6: Ch 3, work 1 dc in each of next 3 sts, 2 dc in next st, * 1 dc in each of next 4 sts, 2 dc in next st, rep from * around, join with SI st to top of beg ch 3 (60 dc).

Rnds 7–11: Ch 3, work 1 dc in each st around, join with Sl st to top of beg ch 3, do not fasten off MC.

Rnds 12 and 13: With CC, ch 1 (counts as sc now and throughout), sk first st, work 1 sc in each st around, join with Sl st to beg ch 1.

Rnds 14 and 15: With MC, rep rnds 12 and 13.

Rnds 16 and 17: With CC, rep rnds 12 and 13, fasten off.

FINISHING

Weave in ends using tapestry needle.

Girl Beanie

The girls like beanies, too, so this one is

styled for them.

YARN

Lightweight wool/acrylic
blend yarn in two colours

Shown: Salsa DK by Sirdar,
50% merino wool/50% acrylic,
1.75 oz (50 g)/162 yd (149 m):
Bright Orange #729, 1 ball
(MC); Bright Blue #727, 1 ball
(CC)

HOOK

9/I (5.5 mm)

STITCHES USED

Single crochet

Double crochet

GAUGE

12 dc = 4" (10 cm)

NOTION

Tapestry needle

FINISHED SIZE

20" to 22" (51 to 56 cm)
head circumference

Lightweight wool/acrylic blend yarn in double crochet.

CAP

Foundation rnd: Using MC, ch 4, join with Sl st to form ring.

Rnd 1: Ch 3 (counts as dc now and throughout), work 9 dc in ring, join with Sl st to top of beg ch 3.

Rnd 2: Ch 3, work 1 dc in same st as ch 3, 2 dc in each rem st around, join with Sl st to top of beg ch 3 (20 dc).

Rnd 3: Ch 3, work 2 dc in next st, * 1 dc in next st, 2 dc in next st, rep from * around, join with Sl st to top of beg ch 3 (30 dc).

Rnd 4: Ch 3, work 1 dc in next st, 2 dc in next st, * 1 dc in each of next 2 sts, 2 dc in next st, rep from * around, join with Sl st to top of beg ch 3 (40 dc).

Rnd 5: Ch 3, work 1 dc in each of next 2 sts, 2 dc in next st, * 1 dc in each of next 3 sts, 2 dc in next st, rep from * around, join with Sl st to top of beg ch 3 (50 dc).

Rnd 6: Ch 3, work 1 dc in each of next 3 sts, 2 dc in next st, * 1 dc in each of next 4 sts, 2 dc in next st, rep from * around, join with Sl st to top of beg ch 3 (60 dc).

Rnds 7–11: Ch 3, work 1 dc in each st around, join with Sl st to top of beg ch 3, do not fasten off MC.

Rnd 12: With CC, ch 1 (counts as sc now and throughout), sk first st, work 1 sc in each st around, join with Sl st to beg ch 1.

Rnd 13: With MC, rep rnd 12.

Rnds 14–18: Rep rnds 12 and 13, fasten off.

FINISHING
Weave in ends using tapestry needle.

Big Stripes Beanie

This cap has wide stripes and an interesting texture

created by crocheting through the back loop of the

stitches. You can never have enough caps!

YARN

Medium-weight acrylic yarn in three colours

Shown: Canadiana by Patons, 100% acrylic, 3.5 oz (100g)/201 yd (185 m): Light Blue #00029, 1 skein (A); Denim #00303, 1 skein (B); Stonewash #00305, 1 skein (C)

HOOK

9/I (5.5 mm)

STITCHES USED

Single crochet

Double crochet

Double crochet through back loop

GAUGE

12 dc = 4" (10 cm)

NOTION

Tapestry needle

FINISHED SIZE

20" to 22" (51 to 56 cm) head circumference

Medium-weight acrylic yarn in double crochet worked through back loop.

CAP

Foundation rnd: Using A, ch 4, join with Sl st to form ring.

Rnd 1: Ch 3 (counts as dc now and throughout), work 9 dc in ring, join with Sl st to top of beg ch 3.

Rnd 2: Ch 3, working tbl of each st now and throughout, 1 dc in same st as ch 3, 2 dc in each rem st around, join with Sl st to top of beg ch 3 (20 dc).

Rnd 3: Ch 3, work 2 dc in next st, * 1 dc in next st, 2 dc in next st, rep from * around, join with Sl st to top of beg ch 3 (30 dc).

Rnd 4: Ch 3, work 1 dc in next st, 2 dc in next st, * 1 dc in each of next 2 sts, 2 dc in next st, rep from * around, join with Sl st to top of beg ch 3 (40 dc), fasten off A.

Rnd 5: Join B, ch 3, work 1 dc in each of next 2 sts, 2 dc in next st, * 1 dc in each of next 3 sts, 2 dc in next st, rep from * around, join with Sl st to top of beg ch 3 (50 dc).

Rnd 6: Ch 3, work 1 dc in each of next 3 sts, 2 dc in next st, * 1 dc in each of next 4 sts, 2 dc in next st, rep from * around, join with Sl st to top of beg ch 3 (60 dc).

Rnds 7 and 8: Ch 3, work 1 dc in each st around, join with Sl st to top of beg ch 3, fasten off B.

Rnds 9–11: Join C at beg of rnd 9, rep rnd 7, but do not fasten off C.

Rnds 12–18: Ch 1 (counts as sc now and throughout), sk first st, work 1 sc in each st around, join with Sl st to beg ch 1, fasten off C.

FINISHING
Weave in ends using tapestry needle.

Retro Stocking Cap

Stocking caps are back. They're just as much fun now as they were when kids spent their winter afternoons building snowmen and flying down hills on their wooden sleds. Here is a classic striped stocking cap, tassel and all.

YARN

Lightweight wool/acrylic blend yarn in two colours

Shown: Salsa DK by Sirdar, 50% merino wool/50% acrylic, 1.75 oz (50 g)/162 yd (149 m): Bright Blue #727, 1 ball (A); Bright Orange #729, 1 ball (B)

HOOK

6/G (4 mm)

STITCHES USED

Single crochet

Reverse single crochet

GAUGE

16 sc = 4" (10 cm)

NOTIONS

Stitch marker

Tapestry needle

8" (20.5 cm) piece of cardboard

FINISHED SIZE

18" to 20" (46 to 51 cm) head circumference

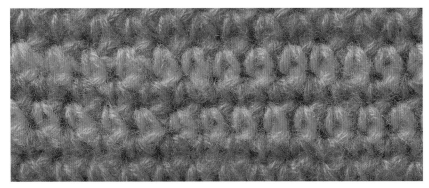

Rows of single crochet in alternating colours form stripes.

CAP

Foundation rnd: Using A, ch 3, join with Sl st to form ring.

Rnd 1: Work 4 sc in ring, pm for beg of rnds, carry marker up at end of each rnd.

Rnd 2: Work 1 sc in each st around.

Rnd 3: Work 2 sc in each st around (8 sc).

Rnds 4–7: Rep rnd 2.

Rnd 8: Work 2 sc in each st around (16 sc), do not fasten off A.

Rnd 9: Join B, work 1 sc in each st around, do not fasten off B.

Rnd 10: With A, work 1 sc in each st around, do not fasten off A.

Rnd 11: With B, work 1 sc in each st around, fasten off B.

Rnds 12–18: With A, work 1 sc in each st around.

Rnds 19–21: Rep rnds 9–11.

Rnd 22: With A, * work 1 sc in next st, 2 sc in next st, rep from * around (24 sc).

Rnds 23–28: Work 1 sc in each st around.

Rnds 29–31: Rep rnds 9–11.

Rnd 32: With A, * work 1 sc in each of next 2 sts, 2 sc in next st, rep from * around (32 sc).

Rnds 33–38: Work 1 sc in each st around.

Rnds 39–41: Rep rnds 9–11.

Rnd 42: With A, * work 1 sc in each of next 3 sts, 2 sc in next st, rep from * around (40 sc).

Rnds 43–48: Work 1 sc in each st around.

Rnds 49–51: Rep rnds 9–11.

Rnds 52–58: With A, work 1 sc in each st around.

Rnds 59–68: Rep rnds 49–58 once.

Rnds 69–77: Rep rnds 49–57.

Rnd 78: With A, * work 1 sc in each of next 4 sts, 2 sc in next st, rep from * around (48 sc).

Rnds 79–81: Rep rnds 9–11.

Rnd 82: With A, * work 1 sc in each of next 5 sts, 2 sc in next st, rep from * around (56 sc).

Rnds 83–87: Work 1 sc in each st around.

Rnd 88: * Work 1 sc in each of next 6 sts, 2 sc in next st, rep from * around (64 sc).

Rnds 89–91: Rep rnds 9–11.

Rnds 92–98: With A, work 1 sc in each st around.

Rnds 99–101: Rep rnds 9–11.

FINISHING

1. After last round, join a strand of A with B and, using both colours, work 1 round reverse single crochet, fasten off and weave in ends using tapestry needle.

2. To create tassel, hold both colours together, and wrap yarn around an 8" (20.5 cm) piece of cardboard about 30 times. Thread a piece of yarn under the loops at the top and tie tightly. Slip the loops off the cardboard. Tie another piece of yarn around the loops 1" (2.5 cm) down from the top. Cut the loops at the other end. Tie the tassel to the cap point.

Tassel adds the finishing touch.

The Newsboy

Extra, extra, read all about it! This is an urban look with lots of attitude. The Newsboy has a great ribbed texture. The reverse side of the stitches is actually on the outside (thanks to Johnny, who told me it looked cooler that way). The ribs are formed by front post double crochet stitches, and the double crochet stitches between the ribs are worked in the spaces rather than the stitches. The bill is worked with two strands of yarn for extra stiffness.

YARN
Bulky-weight wool yarn

Shown: 14 Ply by Wool Pak Yarns NZ, 100% wool, 8 oz (250 g)/310 yd (285 m): Goldstone #27, 1 skein

HOOK
9/I (5.5 mm)

STITCHES USED
Single crochet
Double crochet
Front post double crochet

GAUGE
10 dc = 4" (10 cm)

NOTION
Tapestry needle

FINISHED SIZE
20" to 21" (51 to 53.5 cm) head circumference

61

Ribs formed by front post double crochet stitches; wrong side out.

BILL

Wind off about 12 yd (11 m) of yarn. Hold this yarn together with main skein to crochet bill with a double strand as follows:

Foundation row: Ch 27. Beg in second ch from hook, work 1 sc in each ch to end (26 sc), ch 1, turn.

Rows 1 and 2: Sk first st, * work 1 sc in next st, rep from * across, end 1 sc in tch, ch 1, turn.

Row 3: Sk first st, sc2tog, sc to last 3 sts, sc2tog, sc in last st (24 sc), ch 1, turn.

Row 4: Rep row 3 (22 sc).

Row 5: Rep row 3 (20 sc), fasten off, leaving a long end for sewing. Set cap bill aside.

CAP

Foundation rnd: Ch 4, join with Sl st to form ring, ch 3 (counts as dc now and throughout), work 15 dc in ring (16 dc), join with Sl st to top of ch 3.

Rnd 1: Ch 3, * work 1 FPdc in each of next 2 sts, 1 dc in sp bet last dc worked and next dc (inc made), rep from * 6 times more, 1 FPdc in each of next 2 sts, join with Sl st to top of beg ch 3 (24 dc).

Rnd 2: Ch 3, work 1 dc in next sp, 1 FPdc in each of next 2 FPdc, * 1 dc in next sp, sk dc, 1 dc in next sp, 1 FPdc in each of next 2 FPdc, rep from * 6 times more, join with Sl st to top of beg ch 3 (32 dc).

Rnd 3: Ch 3, work 1 dc in each of next 2 sps, 1 FPdc in each of next 2 FPdc, * 1 dc in each of next 3 sps, 1 FPdc in each of next 2 FPdc, rep from * 6 times more, join with Sl st to top of beg ch 3 (40 dc).

Rnd 4: Ch 3, work 1 dc in each of next 3 sps, 1 FPdc in each of next 2 FPdc, * 1 dc in each of next 4 sps, 1 FPdc in each of next 2 FPdc, rep from * 6 times more, join with Sl st to top of beg ch 3 (48 dc).

Cont to work patt as established, always having 1 more dc bet FPdc ribs, until you have 96 sts.

First dec row: Ch 3, sk 1 sp, dc dec in next 2 sps, 1 dc in each of next 4 sps, 1 dc dec in next 2 sps, 1 dc in next space, 1 FPdc in each of next 2 FPdc, * sk 1 sp, 1 dc next sp, dc dec in next 2 sps, 1 dc in each of next 4 sps, dc dec in next 2 sps, 1 dc in next sp, 1 FPdc in each of next 2 FPdc, rep from * around, join with Sl st to top of beg ch 3 (80 dc).

Second dec row: Ch 3, dc dec in next 2sps, 1 dc in each of next 3 sps, 1 dc dec in next 2 sps, sk 1 sp, 1 FPdc in each of next 2 FPdc, * 1 dc dec in next sp, 1 dc in each of next 3 sps, 1 dc dec in next 2sps, sk 1 sp dec, 2 FPdc, rep from * around (64 sts).

Third dec row: Ch 1, (working each st instead of sp) sk first st, * work 1 sc in each of next 5 sts, sc2tog , rep from * 8 times more (9 dec in all) (55 sts), join with Sl st to beg ch 1, do not fasten off yarn (this is center back of cap).

FINISHING

1. Pin bill to cap front edge, right sides together, matching centers. Sew pieces together using tapestry needle and long yarn that was left, weave in ends.

2. Pick up yarn at center back, sc along bottom of cap, around edge of bill and back to where you started. Join with Sl st, fasten off, weave in ends using tapestry needle.

Super Bulky Hat

Wear this hat on the coldest days of winter. Made from super bulky wool on a large hook, it's quick and easy to make.

YARN

Super bulky weight wool yarn

Shown: Burly Spun by Brown Sheep, 100% wool, 8 oz (226 g)/132 yd (121 m): #BS-59, 1 skein

HOOKS

15/P (10 mm)

STITCHES USED

Single crochet

GAUGE

9 sc = 4" (10 cm)

NOTIONS

Stitch marker

Tapestry needle

FINISHED SIZE

20" to 21" (51 to 53.5 cm) head circumference

65

Single crochet rounds without increases shape the brim.

Foundation rnd: Ch 6, join with Sl st to form ring. Work 6 sc in ring, pm for beg of rnds, carry marker up at end of each rnd.

Rnd 1: Work 2 sc in each st around (12 sc).

Rnd 2: * Work 1 sc in next st, 2 sc in next st (inc made), rep from * around (18 sc).

Rnd 3: * Work 1 sc in each of next 2 sts, 2 sc in next st, rep from * around (24 sc).

Rnd 4: * Work 1 sc in each of next 3 sts, 2 sc in next st, rep from * around (30 sc).

Rnd 5: * Work 1 sc in each of next 4 sts, 2 sc in next st, rep from * around (36 sc).

Rnd 6: * Work 1 sc in each of next 5 sts, 2 sc in next st, rep from * around (42 sc).

Rnd 7: * Work 1 sc in each of next 6 sts, 2 sc in next st, rep from * around (48 sc).

Rnd 8: * Work 1 sc in next st, rep from * around (48 sc). Mark this rnd for start of brim.

Rep rnd 8 until brim is 3" (7.5 cm), fasten off, weave in ends using tapestry needle. Roll up brim.

Cozy Baby Hat

A baby hat is such a perfect newborn gift that I

couldn't resist including just one. This is a super-

soft hat with earflaps and a twist on top.

YARN

Lightweight alpaca yarn in two colours

Shown: Indiecita Baby Alpaca DK by Plymouth, 100% superfine baby alpaca, 1.75 oz (50 g)/125 yd (115 m): #3425, 1 skein (A); #100, 1 skein (B)

HOOKS

5/F (3.75 mm)

6/G (4 mm)

STITCHES USED

Single crochet

Single crochet through back loop

Double crochet

Reverse single crochet

GAUGE

9 clusters = 4" (10 cm) using 6/G hook

6 rows of band = 1" (2.5 cm) using 5/F hook

NOTION

Tapestry needle

FINISHED SIZE

14" (35.5 cm)
head circumference

Shell-stitch rows in alternating colours form the crown.

HAT

Begin with bottom band as follows:

Foundation row: Using 5/F hook and A, ch 11. Starting in second ch from hook, work 1 sc in each ch to end (10 sc), ch 1 (counts as sc now and throughout), turn.

Row 1: Working tbl, sk first st, work 1 sc in each st across.

Rep row 1 for 84 rows, do not fasten off.

Still using A, pick up 72 sc, evenly spaced, along row ends (long side of band). This will be RS of your work. Ch 1, turn.

Change to 6/G hook and work patt as foll:

Foundation row: Sk first st, work 1 sc in next st, * 1 sc, 1 dc in next st, sk 1, rep from * across, ending 1 sc in tch, ch 2, turn.

Row 1: * Work [1 sc, 1 dc] in next st, rep from * 33 times, end 1 dc in tch (34 CL), ch 1, turn.

Row 2: Work 1 dc in same st as tch, * [1 sc, 1 dc] in next st, rep from * 34 times, end 1 sc in tch (35 CL), do not fasten off A, join B.

Rep rows 1 and 2, alternating A and B every two rows for 12 more rows, ch 1, turn. Fasten off B and complete top shaping with A as foll:

Row 1: * Sc in each of next 8 sts, sc2tog, rep from * across, end 1 sc (65 sts), ch 1, turn.

Row 2: Sk first st, sc in each of next 2 sts, sc2tog, * sc in each of next 5 sts, sc2tog, rep from * across, end 5 sc (56 sts), ch 1, turn.

Row 3: Sk first st, sc2tog, * sc in each of next 3 sts, sc2tog, rep from * across (45 sts), ch 1, turn.

Row 4: Sk first st, sc2tog, * sc in each of next 3 sts, sc2tog, rep from * across (36 sts), ch 1, turn.

Row 5: Sk first st, sc2tog, * sc in each of next 3 sts, sc2tog, rep from * across (29 sts), ch 1, turn.

Row 6: Sk first st, sc2tog, * sc in each of next 3 stitches, sc2tog, rep from * across, end 1 sc (23 sts), ch 1, turn.

Row 7: Sk first st, sc2tog across (12 sts), ch 1, turn.

Row 8: Sc2tog across row, fasten off, leaving long end for sewing.

Single crochet stitches worked through the back loop create a "ribbed" bottom band.

EARFLAPS
Make two.

Foundation row: With A, ch 13. Starting in second ch from hook, work 1 sc in each ch (12 sc), ch 1, turn.

Row 1: Sk first st, work 1 sc in each st across, ch 1, turn.

Rows 2, 3, and 4: Rep row 1.

Row 5: Sk first st, sc2tog, sc to last 3 sts, sc2tog, sc in last st, ch 1, turn.

Row 6: Rep row 1.

Cont to rep rows 5 and 1 until 4 sts rem, sc2tog twice, turn, sc2tog, fasten off, leaving long end for sewing.

TOP TWISTS
Make 4.

Using double strand of any leftover yarn, ch 25, turn, work 2 sc in each ch, fasten off, leaving a long end to attach to top of hat.

FINISHING

1. Sew the back seam of the hat, using a tapestry needle and the long yarn that was left, weave in end.

2. Fold the bottom band in half to the inside, and sew in place, weave in end.

3. With B and 5/F hook, work 1 row sc into bottom fold of band, do not turn. Work 1 row rev sc around bottom of hat, fasten off, weave in end.

4. Sew the earflaps in place under the reverse crochet row using long yarn that was left, leaving 1" (2.5 cm) space on each side of the back seam. Weave in ends.

5. With B and 5/F hook, starting at top corner of one earflap, RS facing you, pick up 14 sc down to point, ch 45 for tie, work sc up the ch sts, then cont on other side of earflap, fasten off, weave in ends. Rep for the other earflap.

6. Sew twists to top of hat.

Lion's Mane Hood

This fun-fur hood with pom-poms is warm and

sexy. The project goes fast, since it's made with

large hooks.

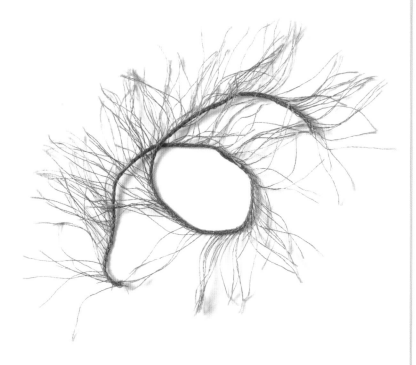

YARN
Bulky-weight novelty fur yarn

Shown: Fun Fur by Lion Brand, 100% polyester, 1.75 oz (50 g)/ 60 yd (55 m): Copper #134, 4 balls

Bulky-weight acrylic/wool blend yarn

Shown: Wool-Ease Chunky by Lion Brand, 80% acrylic/20% wool, 5 oz (142 g)/153 yd (140 m): Pumpkin #133, 1 skein

HOOKS
15/P (10 mm)
9/I (5.5 mm)

STITCH USED
Single crochet

GAUGE
7 sc = 4" (10 cm) on 15/P hook

NOTIONS
Tapestry needle
3" (7.5 cm) square of cardboard

FINISHED SIZE
20" to 22" (51 to 56 cm) head circumference

Bulky-weight acrylic/wool blend yarn in single crochet edges the hood.

HOOD

Fur yarn is used double strand throughout.

Foundation row: Starting at bottom back of neck, with eyelash yarn and 15/P hook, ch 6. Work 1 sc in second ch from hook, 1 sc in each ch (5 sc), ch 1, turn.

Row 1: Sk first st, work 1 sc in each st across, ch 1, turn.

Rows 2, 3, and 4: Rep row 1.

Row 5: Sk first st, work 2 sc in next st (inc made), sc to last 2 sts, inc 1, 1 sc in last st (7 sc), ch 1, turn.

Rows 6, 7, and 8: Rep row 1.

Row 9: Rep row 5 (9 sc).

Rows 10, 11, and 12: Rep row 1.

Row 13: Rep row 5 (11 sc).

Rows 14, 15, and 16: Rep row 1. At end of row 16, do not turn, ch 17 sts, turn.

Starting in second ch from hook, sc in each added ch, cont sc in next 11 sts, ch 17 on other side, turn.

Starting in second ch from hook, sc in each added ch, cont sc to end (43 sc)—16 new sts have been added on each side of center panel of 11 sts.

Cont working in sc on all 43 sts for 7" (18 cm) more, fasten off, weave in ends using tapestry needle.

POM-POMS
Make two.

Cut a piece of eyelash yarn about 18" (46 cm) long, for tying pompom; set aside. Cut 3" (7.5 cm) square of firm cardboard. Wrap yarn 120 times around cardboard. Carefully remove wraps from cardboard, and tie securely in center. Cut lps, shake out and trim to form ball.

FINISHING
1. Hat is T-shaped piece. Fold the horizontal extensions down to meet the vertical sides of the center panel. Sew the edges together.
2. Using 9/I hook and Chunky yarn, leaving a long end to tie on pom-pom, ch 50. Join to left front bottom of hat, continue in sc all around front edge of hat to bottom right front, continue in sc along neck edge back to left front bottom, ch 1, turn. Work a second row back along neck edge. When you reach right front bottom, ch 50, fasten off, leaving a long end to tie on pom-pom.
3. Tie pom-poms to ends of chains.

Cotton Candy
Scarf Hat

It's a scarf, it's a hat, it's both. This

fluffy creation is crocheted in luxurious

mohair yarn in an open pattern.

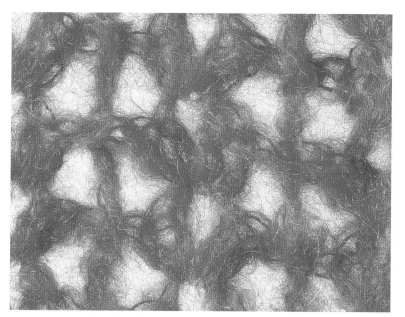
Lacy open-work pattern of double crochet shells and triple crochet stitches.

Make two pieces.

Foundation row: Starting at top, ch 26. Starting in fifth ch from hook, * work 2 dc, ch 2, 2 dc in same ch, sk 2 ch, 1 tr in next ch, sk 2 ch, rep from * until 3 ch rem, sk 2 ch, 1 tr in last ch, ch 4, turn.

Row 1: * Work 2 dc, ch 2, 2 dc in next ch-2 sp, 1 FPtr over bar of tr of prev row, rep from * across, end 1 tr in top of tch, ch 4, turn.

Rep row 1 for 36" (91.5 cm), fasten off.

FINISHING
Using tapestry needle, sew pieces together at top and 10" (25.5 cm) down back. Weave in ends.

COTTON CANDY SCARF HAT

YARN
Bulky mohair yarn

Shown: Ingenua by Katia, 78% mohair/13% polyamide/9% wool, 1.75 oz (50 g)/153 yd (140 m): 1 ball

HOOK
10½/K (6.5 mm)

STITCHES USED
Double crochet
Triple crochet
Front post triple crochet

GAUGE
2 shells 2 tr = 4" (10 cm)

NOTION
Tapestry needle

FINISHED SIZE
10" × 36" (25.5 × 91.5 cm) head circumference

Peruvian Hat

This colourful, warm ski hat is an intermediate-level crochet project. The stripes are worked vertically, and all the colours except the bright accent stripe (colour D) can be carried loosely up the sides as you go along. Add tassels to the flaps if you like.

YARN

Lightweight wool yarn in five colours

Shown: Cleckheaton Country by Plymouth, 100% wool, 1.75 oz (50 g)/104 yd (95 m): Light Blue #1935, 1 skein (A); Turquoise #2230, 1 skein (B); Periwinkle #1548, 1 skein (C); Orange #2167, 1 skein (D); Dark Purple #0288, 1 skein (E)

HOOK

8/H (5 mm)

STITCHES USED

Single crochet

Single crochet through back loop

Double crochet

Popcorn

GAUGE

10 sc and 20 rows = 4" (10 cm)

NOTIONS

Stitch marker

Tapestry needle

3½ (9 cm) piece of cardboard

FINISHED SIZE

20" to 21" (51 to 53.5 cm) head circumference

Alternating stripes of single crochet and popcorn stitches.

HAT

Foundation row (WS): Using A, ch 22. Starting in second ch from hook, work 1 sc in each ch to end (21 sc), ch 1, turn.

Row 1: Sk first st, sc in each st across, ch 1, turn.

Row 2 (pc row, worked from WS): Sk first st, work 1 sc in each of next 2 sts, * pc in next st, sc in each of next 3 sts, rep from * across, end last rep with sc in top of tch (5 pc, 3 sc at beg, and bet each pc, 1 sc at end of row), pull up B in last lp, ch 1 with B, turn.

Row 3: With B, sk first st, work 1 sc in each st across row, 1 sc in top of tch, ch 1, turn.

Row 4: Sk first st, work 1 sc in each st across, 1 sc in top of tch, turn. Pull up C in last lp, ch 1 with C, do not end A.

Row 5: With C, sk first st, work 1 sc tbl only in each st across, ch 1, turn.

Row 6: Sk first st, work 1 sc in each st across, pull up B in last st, do not end C, ch 1 with B, turn.

Row 7: With B, sk first st, work 1 sc in each st across, 1 sc in top of tch, ch 1, turn.

Row 8: Rep row 2, except pull up E in last st, do not end B, turn.

Rows 9–20: Rep rows 3 and 4, alternating colors E, C, E, A, D, B every other row. When changing yarns, fasten off only yarn D. At end of row 20, pull up C in last lp, ch 1 with C, turn.

Row 21: With C, rep row 3.

Row 22: With C, rep row 2, pull up E in last lp, do not end C, ch 1 with E, turn.

Rows 23–30: Rep rows 3 and 4, alternating colors E, A, B, A, every other row.

Rep rows 1–30 twice more (90 rows in all), fasten off.

Using tapestry needle, sew back seam.

CROWN

Rnd 1: With RS facing, starting at top seam, join C, working in sc, work 1 rnd, picking up 1 sc every other row (45 sc), pm in work to mark beg of rnds.

Rnd 2: Work 1 sc in each st around.

Rnd 3: * Work 1 sc in each of next 2 sts, sc2tog, rep from * around, end 1 sc (34 sc).

Rnd 4: * Work 1 sc in next st, sc2tog, rep from * around, end 1 sc (23 sc).

Rnd 5: * Sc2tog, rep from * around, end 1 sc (11 sc), fasten off, leaving long end for sewing.

Using tapestry needle, gather top, sew securely, fasten off.

Using C, work 1 row sc around bottom of hat, set aside.

Shell pattern finishes edge of hat and earflaps.

EARFLAPS
Make two.

With B, ch 17. Work 4 rows sc, then dec 1 st each side every other row until 4 sts rem. Ch 1, turn, sc2tog, 1 sc, ch 1 turn, pick up lp in each of next 2 sts, work off all 3 lps tog. Fasten off B.

With D, starting at top corner, with RS facing, work sc down to point, 3 sc in point to turn, sc back to top, fasten off

TASSELS
Using 1 strand of each color, wind yarn around a 3¹/₂" (9 cm) piece of cardboard once, tie at top, leaving a long end to attach to bottom of earflaps. Tie ¹/₂" (1.3 cm) down from first tie, leaving a long enough end to become part of the tassel.

FINISHING
1. Sew earflaps in place at bottom of hat, leaving 2" (5 cm) space at center back.
2. With C, starting at back seam, work 1 row sc along back, down one side of earflap, 3 sc in corner, up other side of earflap, along front edge of hat,

around other earflap, continuing back to where you started. Do not fasten off, do not turn.

3. Continuing along sts previously worked, work shell patt as foll: * Sk 1 st, work 3 dc in next st, sk 1 st, 1 sc next st, rep from * around bottom of hat and earflaps.

4. Weave in all ends and tie tassels to bottom of earflaps.

Crochet Stitches

SLIP KNOT AND CHAIN

All crochet begins with a chain, into which is worked the foundation row for your piece. To make a chain, start with a slip knot. To make a slip knot, make a loop several inches from the end of the yarn, insert the hook through the loop and catch the tail with the end **(1).** Draw the yarn through the loop on the hook **(2).** After the slip knot, start your chain. Wrap the yarn over the hook (yarn over) and catch it with the hook. Draw the yarn through the loop on the hook. You have now made 1 chain.

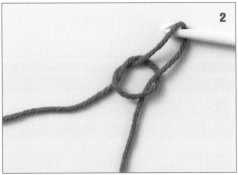

Repeat the process to make a row of chains. When counting chains, do not count the slip knot at the beginning or the loop that is on the hook **(3).**

SLIP STITCH

The slip stitch is a very short stitch, which is mainly used to join two pieces of crochet together when working in rounds. To make a slip stitch, insert the hook into the specified stitch, wrap the yarn over the hook **(1)** and then draw the yarn through the stitch and the loop already on the hook **(2).**

SINGLE CROCHET

Insert the hook into the specified stitch, wrap the yarn over the hook and draw the yarn through the stitch so there are 2 loops on the hook **(1).** Wrap the yarn over the hook again and draw the yarn through both loops **(2).** When working in single crochet, always insert the hook through both top loops of the next stitch, unless the directions specify front loop or back loop only.

SINGLE CROCHET TWO STITCHES TOGETHER

This decreases the number of stitches in a row or round by 1. Insert the hook into the specified stitch, wrap the yarn over the hook and draw the yarn through the stitch so there are 2 loops on the hook **(1).** Insert the hook through the next stitch, wrap the yarn over the hook and draw the yarn through the stitch so there are 3 loops on the hook **(2).** Wrap the yarn over the hook again and draw the yarn through all the loops at once.

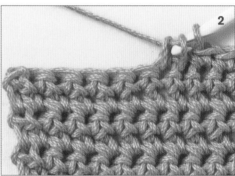

SINGLE CROCHET THROUGH THE BACK LOOP

This creates a distinct ridge on the side facing you. Insert the hook through the back loop only of each stitch, rather than under both loops of the stitch. Complete the single crochet as usual.

REVERSE SINGLE CROCHET

This stitch is usually used to create a border. At the end of a row, chain 1 but do not turn. Working backward, insert the hook into the previous stitch **(1)**, wrap the yarn over the hook and draw the yarn through the stitch so there are 2 loops on the hook. Wrap the yarn over the hook again and draw the yarn through both loops. Continue working in the reverse direction **(2)**.

HALF DOUBLE CROCHET

Wrap the yarn over the hook, insert the hook into the specified stitch and wrap the yarn over the hook again **(1).** Draw the yarn through the stitch so there are 3 loops on the hook. Wrap the yarn over the hook and draw it through all 3 loops at once **(2).**

DOUBLE CROCHET

Wrap the yarn over the hook, insert the hook into the specified stitch and wrap the yarn over the hook again. Draw the yarn through the stitch so there are 3 loops on the hook **(1)**. Wrap the yarn over the hook again and draw it through 2 of the loops so there are now 2 loops on the hook **(2)**. Wrap the yarn over the hook again and draw it through the last 2 loops **(3)**.

DOUBLE CROCHET TWO STITCHES TOGETHER

This decreases the number of stitches in a row or round by 1. Wrap the yarn over the hook, insert the hook into the specified stitch and wrap the yarn over the hook again. Draw the yarn through the stitch so there are 3 loops on the hook. Wrap the yarn over the hook again and draw in through 2 of the loops so there are now 2 loops on the hook. Wrap the yarn over the hook and pick up a loop in the next stitch, so there are now 4 loops on the hook. Wrap the yarn over the hook and draw through 2 loops, yarn over and draw through 3 loops to complete the stitch.

DOUBLE CROCHET THROUGH THE BACK LOOP

This creates a distinct ridge on the side facing you. Wrap the yarn over the hook and insert the hook through the back loop only of each stitch, rather than under both loops of the stitch. Complete the double crochet as usual.

TRIPLE CROCHET

Wrap the yarn over the hook twice, insert the hook into the specified stitch, and wrap the yarn over the hook again. Draw the yarn through the stitch so there are 4 loops on the hook. Wrap the yarn over the hook again **(1)** and draw it through 2 of the loops so there are now 3 loops on the hook **(2).** Wrap the yarn over the hook again and draw it through 2 of the loops so there are now 2 loops on the hook **(3).** Wrap the yarn over the hook again and draw it through the last 2 loops **(4).**

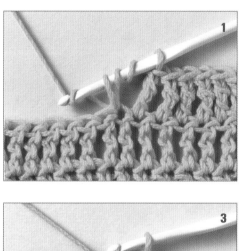

POPCORN STITCH 1

(Worked from the wrong side): Wrap the yarn over the hook, pick up a loop in the next stitch, yarn over and through 2 loops **(1)**. [Wrap the yarn over the hook, pick up a loop in the same stitch, yarn over and through 2 loops] 2 times. Wrap the yarn over the hook and draw it through all 4 loops on the hook **(2)**.

FRONT POST DOUBLE CROCHET

This stitch follows a row of double crochet.

Chain 3 to turn. Wrap the yarn over the hook. Working from the front, insert the hook from right to left (left to right for left-handed crocheters) under the post of the first double crochet from the previous row, and pick up a loop (shown). Wrap the yarn over the hook and complete the stitch as a double crochet.

Left-handed.   Right-handed.

FRONT POST TRIPLE CROCHET

Wrap the yarn over the hook twice. Working from the front, insert the hook from right to left (left to right for left-handed crocheters) under the post of the indicated stitch in the row below, and pick up a loop (shown). Wrap the yarn over the hook and complete the triple crochet stitch as usual.

Left-handed.

Right-handed.

Abbreviations

approx	approximately	**patt**	pattern
beg	begin/beginning	**pc**	popcorn
bet	between	**pm**	place marker
BL	back loop(s)	**prev**	previous
BP	back post	**rem**	remain/remaining
BPdc	back post double crochet	**rep**	repeat(s)
CC	contrasting colour	**rev sc**	reverse single crochet
ch	chain	**rnd(s)**	round(s)
ch-	refers to chain or space previously made, e.g., ch-1 space	**RS**	right side(s)
ch lp	chain loop	**sc**	single crochet
ch-sp	chain space	**sc2tog**	single crochet 2 stitches together
CL	cluster(s)	**sk**	skip
cm	centimetre(s)	**Sl st**	slip stitch
cont	continue	**sp(s)**	space(s)
dc	double crochet	**st(s)**	stitch(es)
dc2tog	double crochet 2 stitches together	**tch**	turning chain
dec	decrease/decreases/decreasing	**tbl**	through back loop
FL	front loop(s)	**tog**	together
foll	follow/follows/following	**tr**	triple crochet
FP	front post	**WS**	wrong side(s)
FPdc	front post double crochet	**yd**	yard(s)
FPtr	front post triple crochet	**yo**	yarn over
g	gram(s)	**yoh**	yarn over hook
hdc	half double crochet	**[ ]**	Work instructions within brackets as many times as directed
inc	increase/increases/increasing	**( )**	At end of row, indicates total number of stitches worked
lp(s)	loop(s)	*****	Repeat instructions following the single asterisk as directed
m	metre(s)	******	Repeat instructions between asterisks as many times as directed or repeat from a given set of instructions
MC	main color		
mm	millimetre(s)		
oz	ounce(s)		
p	picot		